VERDURE

VERDURE

VEGETABLE RECIPES FROM
THE AMERICAN ACADEMY IN ROME

———

BY CHRISTOPHER BOSWELL

WITH ELENA GOLDBLATT

———

PHOTOGRAPHY BY ANNIE SCHLECHTER

ROME
SUSTAINABLE
FOOD
PROJECT

The Little Bookroom

New York

Library of Congress Cataloging-in-Publication Data
is on file at the Library of Congress

Printed in the United States of America

Published by The Little Bookroom
435 Hudson Street, Suite 300
New York NY 10014
editorial@littlebookroom.com
www.littlebookroom.com

ISBN 978-1-936941-03-2

10 9 8 7 6 5 4 3 2 1

TABLE OF CONTENTS

FOREWORD

It is difficult to speak of Italian food as a whole since the nation's regional culinary traditions are so engrained. I would argue that Italy has a greater diversity of cuisines than any other country in the world. To me, this is what makes Italian cooking unique. Italy remains a divided country in which each region—each town, in fact—has its own culinary customs based on climate, historical traditions, and even politics. For example, bread in Umbria and Tuscany is still made without a trace of salt because of a tax imposed on salt during the Middle Ages.

Yet these culinary differences share a common foundation: vegetables, which are truly at the heart of all Italian cuisine. I would also venture to say that nowhere else will you feel the profound respect and reverence that Italians demonstrate toward their produce. This is why I love cooking Italian food, and specifically why I adore cooking vegetables in Italy.

Italian food is known for the extraordinary flavor created by a simple set of ingredients. This unadorned cuisine is rooted in *la cucina povera*, the "food of the poor," that developed in a predominantly agricultural country. For centuries, Italian peasants survived on what the land had to offer. Poverty and need led to great innovation and creativity; peasants across the country developed a vast repertoire of wholesome and uncomplicated dishes.

At the Rome Sustainable Food Project (RSFP) we strive to share the delicious and simple recipes of *la cucina povera*, and to celebrate the amazing bounty of vegetables that are the foundation of almost any Italian meal. Our goal is to maintain these traditions. We provide the community of the American Academy in Rome with a daily Mediterranean diet that relies heavily on a wide variety of seasonal vegetables, fortified with grains, eggs, cheese, small amounts of meat, and even smaller amounts of fish. We seek to pay tribute to modern farmers' respect for the seasonality and integrity of vegetables, and to foster our everyday relationship with these farmers. *Verdure* strives to reaffirm our connection with the food we eat in a world that has largely become disconnected with the sources of its food. Our mission is not only to teach future cooks, but also to inspire an entire community to cook, eat, and share seasonal food without ever needing to stray out of season.

Christopher Boswell
Rome

VEGETABLES IN THE RSFP KITCHEN

When Alice Waters founded the Rome Sustainable Food Project in 2007, she, Mona Talbott, and I knew that we weren't going to simply change the food at the American Academy: we were going to revolutionize it. We were going to create a local, seasonal, organic, and sustainable kitchen to provide meals for the community of artists and scholars. The goal of the RSFP was to bring people to the table and encourage a true cross-pollination and exchange of ideas over delicious and nourishing food. *Verdure*, or vegetables, were at the heart of this food revolution.

Vegetables are the backbone of the RSFP kitchen and are a part of virtually every dish. The interns of the RSFP and the community of the American Academy are always struck by the quantity and diversity of the vegetables we offer. Year round, from just 14 raised beds, we harvest more than 6,000 pounds of fruits and vegetables that are started from seed. Nothing in our kitchen goes to waste: we compost all our vegetable scraps and use the compost to enrich the soil of our vegetable garden.

Each day, we serve a buffet lunch and a seated dinner. Lunch includes a soup, a pasta or risotto, and four to five different vegetable-based side dishes. Dinner is always a served three-course meal. We often serve dinner "family style," from communal platters, which the community passes to represent the camaraderie and conviviality we seek to foster. This means that each day six out of the eight dishes served for lunch and dinner are vegetable dishes. In other words, 42 of the 52 different dishes a week (excluding desserts) are purely vegetarian or vegetable-based side dishes.

Our dishes at the Rome Sustainable Food Project are inspired by a deep respect for *la cucina povera* as well as Roman and Italian traditions, in which vegetables are the centerpiece. I am always humbled when Italian visitors comment on the authenticity of the Italian dishes we cook. This truly is an extraordinary compliment coming from an Italian. I am equally grateful for how enthusiastic they are about our California-inspired reinterpretations of traditional Italian dishes that we learned in our years cooking at Chez Panisse. Italians are a tough crowd and their fierce loyalty to the simplicity of tradition makes their appreciation of our creative repertoire all the more meaningful.

While *Verdure* is really a collection of Italian *contorni,* or side dishes, we believe that many can stand on their own as a main course. They can also be combined to make a wonderful mixed antipasto. All the recipes are designed to serve 4 to 6 people.

MICROSEASONALITY

One of the most important lessons that Alice Waters taught me at Chez Panisse was to recognize that the same vegetable requires different preparations at different times throughout the year.

This is what we mean when we talk about microseasonality in the following recipes: the short seasons of fruits and vegetables within their larger season. Microseasonality is really about the difference in the vegetable at the beginning, middle, and end of its season. This determines not only *what* you will cook, but also *how* you will cook your ingredients in order to maximize their flavor.

As a general rule, early-season vegetables, what Romans call *primizie,* need to be cooked less because they tend to be sweeter and more tender. However, as the season progresses and the vegetable changes in size, color, texture, and flavor, you must also change your cooking approach. At the end of the season, you may need to salt eggplant to extract bitterness before cooking it; cucumbers and fava beans may need to be peeled as the season evolves. In most cases, you will probably need to cook the vegetables for a longer period of time as they become tougher or starchier. Ultimately, the state of the vegetable decides the preparation, and you, the cook, must respond in a way that maximizes its natural flavor while doing as little as possible to alter it, so that it always remains the star of the dish.

A final note: You can't ever really know where vegetables have been and what they have been exposed to. Whether you buy clean-looking (even "washed") vegetables at a supermarket or dirt-encrusted vegetables at a farmers' market, I always recommend washing all vegetables thoroughly, perhaps two or even three times, before using them; that's the only way to be sure they're truly clean.

AUTUNNO

AUTUNNO
AUTUMN

Every September, I am thrilled to be back at the American Academy after the summer break and to be cooking again as the weather cools and autumn begins. In my opinion, fall is by far the best time to cook and to teach the interns, since it is truly a crossroads between summer and winter when a greater number of different fruits and vegetables are available than at any other time of the year.

In Rome, summer's bounty extends far into October. As the weather gets colder, late summer produce overlaps with the first fall fruits: sweet fall figs, persimmons, and pomegranates complement the first cold-weather chicories (radicchio, escarole, and endive), which are bitter. In such a temperate climate you can even get fresh *peperoncino* as late as December, along with the hearty vegetables of winter.

Microseasonality, or "seasons within seasons," is especially apparent during the fall. As seasons evolve, produce needs to be treated differently. This is why fall is the most interesting time to cook and the best time to learn: a vegetable in late summer may be very different than the same vegetable in early fall, so you need to know various ways of cooking an ingredient in order to bring out its best at any given time within its season.

As summer ends, eggplant and zucchini begin to get bitter, so for this reason eggplant often has to be salted and drained in the fall to extract its bitter juices. In fall the seedy pulp of zucchini has to be scooped out before consumption, while in summer this usually isn't necessary. By the beginning of fall, tomatoes become intensely sweet and peppers are bold and pungent. These thick-skinned vegetables aren't as good raw as they were in early summer; they are now better suited to being cooked in stews and sauces.

Another wonderful thing about the autumn, I think, is that the days still tend to be warm while the evenings are cool, allowing us to cook such a variety of dishes within the same day: lighter more summery dishes during the day and heartier, richer, dishes at night to keep us warm. There's no two ways about it: I just love the fall.

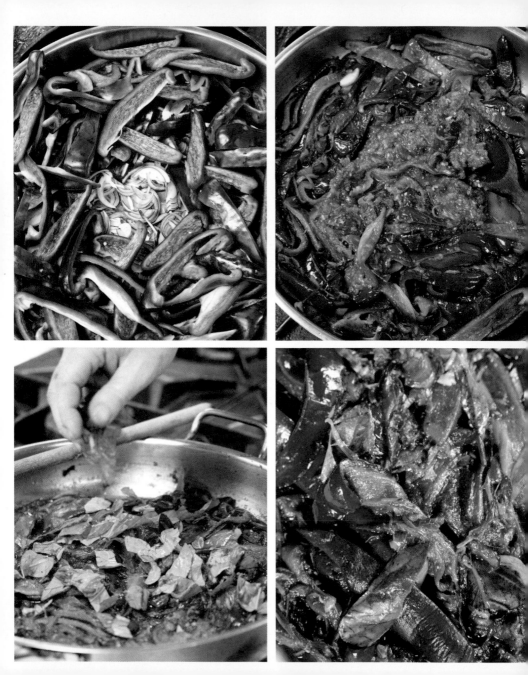

PEPERONATA
ITALIAN-STYLE STEWED PEPPERS

This dish is so versatile: amazing on its own, it also goes well with sausages, polenta, poached eggs, mozzarella...the list goes on. At the RSFP we prepare peperonata in the summer and in the fall, but it really is at its very best around September, made with peppers that have ripened all summer in bountiful sunshine. The tomato puree may be replaced with tomato confit or tomato paste (use a smaller amount of paste). We often use whatever types of tomatoes we have on hand, and I encourage you to cook in the same spontaneous way.

⅓ cup (79 ml) extra virgin olive oil

6 garlic cloves, peeled and smashed

2 large red onions, peeled and thinly sliced

8 red or yellow bell peppers, cut into ⅓-inch (.8-cm) strips

1 cup tomato puree from canned whole San Marzano-style tomatoes, pureed with a hand blender or in a food processor

20 Italian basil leaves

3 tablespoons red wine vinegar

1 teaspoon hot pepper flakes

Put the olive oil in a deep high-sided pot. Begin to build the peperonata in layers by first scattering the garlic, then adding the onions in an even layer, and finally adding the peppers.

Place the pot over medium heat and do not stir the peppers. When you begin to hear a slight sizzling sound and the onions start to become translucent, stir the peperonata for the first time and keep stirring it occasionally as it cooks.

After about 20 minutes the peppers should begin to soften. Add the tomato puree and cook for another 15 minutes, or until the peppers are tender.

Add the basil, vinegar, and hot pepper. Taste and adjust the seasoning with salt and more vinegar if necessary. Serve hot or at room temperature.

PEPERONI ALLA SALERNITANA
STEWED PEPPERS WITH FRIED POTATOES & BASIL

Peperoni alla Salernitana is originally from Salerno on the Amalfi Coast. This is the RSFP version: a crunchy, sweet, sour, herby side dish. Try serving it with roasted pork—the combination is brilliant. Make sure the potatoes are fully dry before frying them or they will splatter when they hit the hot oil.

4 medium Yukon gold potatoes, peeled and cut into ½-inch (1.3-cm) dice (keep in cold water until needed)

¼ cup (59 ml) extra virgin olive oil

4 garlic cloves, peeled and smashed

6 large red bell peppers, cut into ½-inch (1.3-cm) dice

20 Italian basil leaves

1 to 2 tablespoons red wine vinegar

3 quarts (2.8 l) vegetable oil

Bring a medium pot of cold water to a boil.

When the water comes to a rolling boil, salt it, and cook the potatoes for 10 minutes, or until tender and smashed easily with a fork. Drain them and spread the potatoes out on baking sheet to cool.

Put the olive oil, garlic, and peppers in a large sauté pan over medium heat. Do not stir. When the peppers begin to make a slight sizzling sound, stir them. Slowly stew them for about 25 minutes, turning down the heat if they are browning, stirring only occasionally, until they are very tender. Turn off the heat, add the basil, red wine vinegar, and season with salt.

Put the vegetable oil in a medium high-sided pot over medium heat. Make sure the oil does not go more than halfway up the sides of the pot. When the oil reaches 350°F (177°C), carefully add half of the potatoes and fry them for just a few minutes, until crisp and golden. Remove them using a slotted spoon and drain the potatoes on paper towels. Sprinkle with salt and repeat this process with the rest of the potatoes.

Add the hot potatoes to the peppers, stirring carefully, and let sit for 10 minutes before serving.

TORTINO DI PATATE E POMODORI FRESCHI
POTATO & FRESH TOMATO GRATIN

This is one of best gratins you can make when you have an abundance of nice, ripe tomatoes and the weather hasn't yet cooled. Although it is excellent served warm for dinner, it is also delicious served at room temperature for lunch with a nice salad. I prefer to use chicken stock, but it may be prepared with vegetable stock. The trick is cooking it a day ahead so it has time to set, and pressing down the gratin repeatedly into its own juices as it cooks so that it remains moist and the top slowly starts to brown and crisp up.

⅓ cup (79 ml) extra virgin olive oil

2 medium yellow onions, peeled and thinly sliced (about 2 cups)

8 large Russet potatoes, peeled and cut into ¼-inch (.6-cm)-thick slices (keep in cold water until needed)

10 large, ripe and firm Roma tomatoes, cored and cut into ⅛-inch (.3-cm)-thick slices

10 thyme sprigs, picked and chopped (about 1 tablespoon)

2 oz (57 g) Grana Padano or Parmigiano-Reggiano, grated (about ¼ cup)

2 cups (473 ml) chicken broth

Preheat the oven to 350°F (177°C).

Put the olive oil, onions, and a pinch of salt in a 10-inch (25-cm) sauté pan over medium heat. Sweat the onions, stirring occasionally, until they are soft and translucent. Meanwhile, lightly season the potatoes and tomatoes separately.

Add the thyme to the onions. Transfer the onions to a large rectangular baking dish, spreading them evenly on the bottom.

Over the base of onions alternate layers of potatoes, tomatoes, and cheese, finishing with a layer of potatoes.

Add 2 cups of chicken broth and cover the baking dish tightly with aluminum foil. Bake for about 1 hour, checking the potatoes every 30 minutes with a knife until it meets no resistance and the potatoes are tender. Remove the foil and press down using a spatula to bring the juices to the surface, to help brown or "gratin" the top layer. Bake until the top is golden and crispy and almost all the juices have been absorbed, pressing down with the spatula every 15 minutes, for about another hour total. Let cool before serving.

FAGIOLINI CORALLO STRACOTTI

LONG-COOKED ROMANO BEANS

As a kid, this was one of my favorites of the side dishes that my mother made. When I started to cook professionally I assumed that she overcooked the Romano beans, but when I came to Italy, quite to my surprise, I discovered that this dish was cooked the very same way she prepared it. Over the years I have had several versions (including stewed with tomatoes, which is delicious), but this remains my hands-down favorite. I like to think there is a little bit of the Italian grandmother in all of us, even in my American mom. Romano beans are known by a variety of other names: taccole, Italian flat beans, and Roma beans are all essentially the same.

½ cup (118 ml) extra virgin olive oil

6 garlic cloves, peeled and smashed

3 lbs (1.4 kg) Romano beans, tops and tails removed and cut into 2-inch (5-cm) pieces

Freshly ground black pepper, to taste

Put the olive oil, garlic, and Romano beans in a large high-sided pot over medium-low heat and cover almost completely with a lid, leaving just a crack for steam to escape.

After about 20 minutes, stir the beans, and replace the lid as it was before. If the beans are starting to brown, turn the heat to low and add about ½ cup water.

Keep stirring every 15 minutes until the beans are very soft, slightly browning, and sweet. They should be ready after about 1 hour. Salt and pepper if you like and serve immediately.

FAGIOLI BORLOTTI FRESCHI CON PEPERONI ARROSTITI

FRESH BORLOTTI BEAN SALAD WITH ROASTED PEPPERS

———

In late summer and early fall, the Fellows love to come sit with the RSFP interns in the cortile and help us shell mountains of fresh beans. They often comment on how medita-tive shelling beans can be, and we tend to agree. The fantastic rich creaminess of freshly shelled beans is essential to this dish. What's more, they cook in less time than the more commonly used dry beans, and there is no need to soak them overnight. This recipe is quite simple (though a little time-consuming), but you can prepare the peppers and the beans in advance. If you prepare the roasted peppers while the beans cook, this dish is quick and easy to toss together at the last minute.

2 roasted and marinated bell peppers (about half the batch on p. 209)

2 medium shallots or 1 small red onion, peeled and minced

¼ cup (59 ml) red wine vinegar

4 cups cooked fresh Borlotti beans (p. 219)

¼ cup (59 ml) extra virgin olive oil

12 Italian basil leaves, torn

Combine the shallots and the red wine vinegar in a small bowl. Add a pinch of salt and let the shallots macerate for 45 minutes. Transfer the shallots (reserving the vinegar) to the roasted peppers and mix well. Taste and adjust the seasoning using some of the reserved vinegar.

In a large bowl, toss the cooked beans with the olive oil and basil, and season with salt. Add the marinated roasted peppers. Taste and adjust the seasoning, and serve immediately.

FAGIOLINI IN UMIDO ALLO ZAFFERANO
GREEN BEANS STEWED WITH TOMATOES & SAFFRON

This is a great contorno that I learned to make at Chez Panisse, where it is often served with baked white fish. At the RSFP, we rarely cook fish because there is very little sustainably harvested fish in the Mediterranean, so we prefer to make these beans for our lunch buffet. As the weather cools, we serve them at dinner alongside polenta and poached eggs. The key is to stew the tomatoes until they melt into the saffron onions and make a delicious sugo.

10 San Marzano-style tomatoes

¼ cup (59 ml) extra virgin olive oil

2 medium yellow onions, peeled and thinly sliced

1 small pinch saffron threads

1½ lbs (680 g) green beans, topped and tailed

Bring a medium pot of cold water to a boil.

Score the bottom of the tomatoes with an X and core them. Blanch the tomatoes by lowering them, a few at a time, into the boiling water. Let them cook just long enough for the skins to loosen or blister slightly, about 30 seconds. Remove them quickly using a slotted spoon and transfer them to a bowl of ice water. Reserve the water to cook the green beans. Peel off the skins of the tomatoes with your fingers or with a paring knife, and dice the tomatoes.

Put the olive oil and onions in a 12-inch (30-cm) sauté pan over low heat. Add a pinch of salt and the saffron threads. Slowly sweat the onions, stirring occasionally, until they are soft and translucent.

Add the tomatoes and cook for 10 more minutes, or until the tomatoes are soft and juicy. Season with salt.

Salt the boiling tomato water and add the beans. Cook for 6 minutes, or until tender. Drain, then transfer them to the onions and tomatoes. Simmer for 3 more minutes over medium-low heat, taste and adjust the seasoning, and serve immediately.

SCAROLA RIPASSATA IN PADELLA CON UVETTA E PINOLI

SAUTÉED ESCAROLE WITH RAISINS & PINE NUTS

At the RSFP we make a point of using every part of a vegetable. If we prepare an escarole salad, the outer leaves that aren't tender enough to use in the salad are saved and cooked later. This sautéed escarole is of Sicilian origin, and we often make it for lunch because it is an ideal way to use the tough green outer leaves. I particularly love the sweet and sour taste that results when the raisins play against the garlicky bitter greens.

¼ cup raisins or currants

4 tablespoons white wine vinegar

¼ cup pine nuts

½ cup (118 ml) extra virgin olive oil

3 garlic cloves, peeled and smashed

2 lbs (907 g) escarole, washed and cut into 1-inch (2.5-cm)-wide ribbons

Preheat the oven to 300°F (149°C).

In a small pot, combine the raisins, 1½ cups water, and the white wine vinegar. Bring to a boil and turn off the heat. Allow the raisins to plump in the liquid for 25 minutes away from the heat source.

Toast the pine nuts in the oven on a rimmed baking sheet for about 7 minutes, or until they are fragrant and just lightly golden.

Put the olive oil and garlic in a large sauté pan over medium-high heat. When the oil is hot and the garlic is golden, remove and discard the cloves. Add the escarole and sauté, stirring frequently, until it is tender. Remove the raisins from the liquid (reserving it for later). Add the raisins and pine nuts to the pan and continue cooking for another minute. Add some of the raisin liquid if the mixture looks dry. Taste and adjust the seasoning and serve immediately.

BAGNA CAUDA
AUTUMN VEGETABLES
WITH WARM ANCHOVY BUTTER SAUCE

————

The "warm bath" of this recipe's name refers to the warm anchovy-garlic dipping sauce. Originally from Piedmont, the sauce is traditionally served in a small terracotta pot with a votive candle underneath to keep it warm. Some Italians like to boil the garlic in milk to mellow its flavor, but I don't because I prefer the intense garlic taste that matches the bold flavor of the anchovies. This is an especially wonderful antipasto in the fall, because it uses both late summer vegetables and the first cabbage, broccoli, and cauliflower of autumn. Feel free to mix up the vegetables based on season and availability, playing on sweet, salty, and bitter tastes and textures. Barely cooked artichokes, cardoons, turnips, and potatoes are delicious. Sweet vegetables such as carrots or other root vegetables are also perfect, as are bitter greens, radicchio, or vegetables from the broccoli family.

½ cup (118 ml) extra virgin olive oil

4 tablespoons (57 g) butter

5 salt-packed anchovies, cleaned (p. 223) or 10 tinned anchovy fillets in oil

4 garlic cloves, peeled and thinly sliced

½ small head savoy cabbage, cored and cut into wedges

2 carrots, peeled and sliced into ⅛-inch (.3-cm)-thick coins

1 bell pepper, seeded and cut into ⅛-inch (.3-cm)-thick slices

2 cucumbers, peeled and cut into ⅛-inch (.3-cm)-thick slices

10 cherry tomatoes, cut in half

Put the olive oil and butter in a small pot over low heat and cook until the butter has completely melted.

Add the anchovy fillets and the garlic and cook for 5 minutes, or until the anchovy has dissolved into the oil, stirring with a fork to break up the anchovy if necessary. Turn off the heat and let sit for 10 to 15 minutes to infuse the butter and olive oil with the anchovies and garlic.

Place all of the vegetables on a platter (if you like, blanch some of the firmer vegetables first in boiling salted water for just a few minutes). Put the warm anchovy sauce in a small bowl and serve alongside the vegetables.

1 small cauliflower, trimmed and cut into florets

2 celery stalks, cut into 2-inch (5-cm) pieces

*1 fennel bulb, trimmed and cut into
⅛-inch (.3-cm)-thick rings*

INSALATA COMPOSTA DI PORRI, RAPE ROSSE, FINOCCHIO E SALSA DI SENAPE

LEEK, BEET & FENNEL SALAD
WITH CREAMY MUSTARD DRESSING

———

This composed salad has four distinct flavors that are delicious in combination. The sweet leeks, licorice-scented fennel, and earthy beets are complemented and contrasted in every bite by the spicy mustard dressing. At the RSFP, we often garnish this salad with a few leaves of peppery arugula from the Bass Garden. Arugula is in the mustard family, and it gives the dish an extra kick of spiciness. Make sure you discard the tough rubbery outer layer of the leek, and wash the leek coins in plenty of lukewarm water to help dislodge any dirt between the layers.

6 medium beets, roasted, cut into wedges, and marinated (p. 211)

1 batch aïoli (p. 201)

3 tablespoons whole-grain mustard

2 tablespoons Dijon mustard

1 lemon

2 fennel bulbs, trimmed and cut into ½-inch (1.3-cm) wedges

4 small leeks, trimmed and cut into ¼-inch (.6-cm) coins

2 tablespoons extra virgin olive oil

Bring a large pot of cold water to a boil.

In a small bowl, combine both mustards and the aïoli, adjusting the consistency with a little lemon juice and water so that it drizzles easily when poured with a spoon. Taste and adjust the seasoning and let sit for at least 15 minutes.

When the water comes to a rolling boil, salt it, and blanch the fennel for about 5 minutes, or until it is tender but not too soft. Remove it using a slotted spoon and scatter the fennel on a baking sheet to cool. In the same pot of water, blanch the leeks for about 3 minutes, or until they are tender but not too soft. Drain them and scatter the leeks on a baking sheet to cool.

In a medium bowl, toss the leeks and fennel with the olive oil and season with salt. Arrange the leeks and fennel on a platter. Drain the beets and scatter them over the vegetables. Drizzle with the mustard dressing and serve immediately.

FRITTO MISTO DI RAPE ROSSE, CAVOLFIORE E BORRAGINE

FRITTO MISTO OF BEETS, CAULIFLOWER & BORAGE

Fritto misto is a classic Italian appetizer and a great way to start any meal. The key to a good fritto is the temperature of the oil and the consistency of the batter. We use a batter (pastella) that is very easy to make. The secret to a great pastella is keeping it as cold as possible so that when it comes into contact with the hot oil, it puffs up and creates a beautiful fluffy golden crust around the vegetable. Fried marinated beets are particularly delicious and add a nice twist to this dish. They maintain the sweet and sour taste of beets and to top it off they turn the pastella a beautiful purple hue. This is a perfect way to use leftover roasted beets.

4 medium beets, roasted, cut into wedges, and marinated (p. 211)

2 cups (256 g) all-purpose flour

2¼ cups (532 ml) cold seltzer water

½ small head of cauliflower (about 12 oz [340 g]), trimmed and cut into large florets

4 quarts (3.8 l) vegetable oil

6 large borage leaves or Lacinato, Tuscan, or dinosaur kale leaves

1 lemon, optional

Prepare the pastella: whisk the flour and seltzer water together in a medium bowl. Add a pinch of salt and let rest in the freezer for 15 minutes, then transfer it to the refrigerator until you need it.

Bring a large pot of cold water to a boil.

When the water comes to a rolling boil, salt it, and add the cauliflower. Cook for 3 minutes, until just tender. Drain the cauliflower and scatter it on a baking sheet to cool.

Pour the vegetable oil into a medium high-sided pot over medium heat. Make sure the oil does not go more than halfway up the sides of the pot.

When the oil reaches 350°F (177°C), put ⅓ of the pastella from the medium bowl into a small bowl. Use the small bowl to dip the beets and the medium bowl to dip the cauliflower and borage leaves. Working in small batches, delicately dip the vegetables into the batter one by one and carefully lower them into the oil. Make sure the temperature of the oil is consistently at 350°F (177°C). Fry until golden on one side (about 3 minutes) and then flip the vegetables over and cook until golden on the other side.

Remove them using a slotted spoon and place them onto paper towels to drain. Sprinkle with salt and repeat this process with all the vegetables. Serve immediately with lemon wedges, if you like.

INSALATA DI SPINACI
CON PANCETTA E ACETO BALSAMICO
WARM SPINACH SALAD WITH PANCETTA VINAIGRETTE

————

We make this salad with the tender spinach that we grow in the Bass Garden in the fall. We plant spinach as a cover crop when there is a gap in the planting season between summer and winter crops. This warm salad is very nice served for dinner in the early fall, when the Fellows still eat outside in the cortile. It is a lovely first course alternative to a pasta or soup.

2 large shallots or 1 medium red onion, peeled and minced

⅓ cup (79 ml) balsamic vinegar

2 tablespoons red wine vinegar

¼ cup pine nuts

½ cup (118 ml) extra virgin olive oil

4 oz (113 g) pancetta or smoked bacon, cut into ¼-inch (.6-cm) dice

3 garlic cloves, peeled and smashed

¾ lb (340 g) Bloomsdale or baby spinach

Freshly ground black pepper, to taste

Preheat the oven to 300°F (149°C).

Combine the shallots and the balsamic and red wine vinegars in a small bowl. Add a pinch of salt and let the shallots macerate for 45 minutes.

Toast the pine nuts in the oven on a rimmed baking sheet for about 7 minutes, or until they are fragrant and just lightly golden.

Put 2 tablespoons of the olive oil and the pancetta in a medium pot over low heat. Render the pancetta, stirring occasionally, for about 15 minutes, or until it starts to brown. Add the garlic and let sizzle until it is golden, then remove and discard it. Add the vinegars and the shallots, turn the heat to medium high and bring to a boil. Immediately add the remaining olive oil, turn off the heat and leave the vinaigrette on the burner to keep it warm.

In a large bowl toss the spinach with salt, pepper, and some of the pancetta vinaigrette. Taste and adjust the seasoning, adding more vinaigrette as necessary. Top with the pine nuts and serve immediately.

INSALATA DI RADICCHI MISTI CON FRUTTA AUTUNNALE E ACETO BALSAMICO

CHICORIES SALAD WITH FALL FRUITS & BALSAMIC VINEGAR

In this California-inspired salad, persimmons, pears, and pomegranates are combined with the crispy, crunchy, slightly bitter lettuces known as radicchio, a member of the chicory family. Chicories are hearty head lettuces with tough outer leaves that help them resist the cold. As the weather gets colder, the outer leaves of the chicory plant protect its core and inner leaves. These inner leaves are beautiful, crunchy, sweet little lettuces that are wonderfully complemented by a good balsamic vinaigrette and succulent fall fruit. This salad is profoundly satisfying: the combination of textures and of sweet, sour, salty, and bitter flavors is absolutely fantastic.

⅓ cup (79 ml) good quality balsamic vinegar

3 medium shallots or 1 small red onion, peeled and minced

2 lbs (907 g) mixed chicories such as frisée, Chioggia radicchio, Treviso radicchio, and sugar loaf

⅔ cup (158 ml) extra virgin olive oil

1 pear, cut into ⅛-inch (.3-cm)-thick slices

1 fennel bulb, trimmed and very thinly sliced using a knife or a mandoline

1 fuyu persimmon, very thinly sliced using a knife or a mandoline

1 pomegranate, seeded (p. 227)

Freshly ground black pepper, to taste

Put the balsamic vinegar, shallots or onion, and a pinch of salt in a 1-quart (.9-l) measuring cup. Macerate the shallots in the vinegar for 1 hour.

Trim any bitter, dark, or withered outer leaves from the chicories and cut the delicate inner leaves into 1-inch (2.5-cm) strips or tiles. Wash them very well (p. 235) and set them aside in the refrigerator.

Add the olive oil to the vinegar and stir very well using a fork or whisk until the dressing has emulsified.

In a large bowl, combine the pear, fennel, persimmon, pomegranate seeds, and chicories and mix to combine. Season with salt and pepper. Stir the dressing vigorously to obtain an emulsion, then dress the salad. Toss well with your hands, taste and adjust the seasoning, and serve immediately.

INSALATA DI CAVOLO NERO CON MANDORLE TOSTATE E PECORINO

TUSCAN KALE SALAD
WITH TOASTED ALMONDS & PECORINO

Giovanni Guerrera, the sous-chef at the American Academy for the 2011-2012 academic year, was the first person to suggest that we use cavolo nero, or its American equivalent, Tuscan kale, in a salad. Of course this makes total sense because cavolo nero is a member of the cabbage family, but it had just never occurred to me. We like to grow cavolo nero in the Bass Garden in two ways. We seed cavolo nero like arugula, which keeps the plant small and yields several harvests of little leafy cavolo nero that is tender, slightly bitter, delicious, and perfect for this salad. We also grow larger, sturdier cavolo nero, which is traditionally used for cooking. If you're using the large-leaf kind—far easier to find than small-leaf cavolo nero—cut it into bite-sized pieces and dress the cavolo nero ahead of time. The trick here is to really massage the large leaves (which usually is never done to salad greens!) to help them break down and become tender.

1 cup salted toasted almonds, chopped (p. 207)

4 medium carrots, peeled and grated on a box grater, using the large holes, or julienned using a mandoline

2 lemons (about 5 tablespoons lemon juice)

¾ lb (340 g) cavolo nero or Lacinato, Tuscan, or dinosaur kale, sturdy leaves stripped from the stems and cut into ¼-inch (.6-cm) ribbons (small leaves trimmed only)

¼ cup (59 ml) extra virgin olive oil

1½ oz (43 g) chunk of aged pecorino toscano, shaved with a peeler

In a medium bowl, with your hands, massage the carrots with half of the lemon juice and a large pinch of salt. Let sit for 20 minutes so that the carrots become soft.

Toss the cavolo nero in another medium bowl with the olive oil and season with salt (massaging the oil into the leaves if you are using large-leaf cavolo nero). Add the cavolo nero to the marinated carrots and let sit for 5 minutes. Taste and adjust the seasoning, adding more salt or lemon juice as necessary. Top with the chopped almonds and shaved pecorino and serve immediately.

OLIO NUOVO
NEW-HARVEST OLIVE OIL

In late fall, central and southern Italy erupt with the frantic energy needed to harvest olives and press them before the cold weather and heavy rains arrive. Harvesting olives is lots of fun, and there really is nothing better than tasting the warm and pungent olive oil straight from a press the very same day that you harvested the olives. For the past two years during the fall, we have taken the RSFP interns to Madi Gandolfo's house in Umbria; Madi is the Development and External Affairs Officer at the Academy, and she has a large olive grove on her property near the town of Amelia. When we took the olives for this year, the man at the mill told us that our olives were the best ones he'd seen all season. We were all beaming with pride.

Inspired by our Umbrian olive picking, Bass Garden superintendent Alessandra Vinciguerra and I decided to organize a collaborative harvesting of the olive trees in the garden with the gardeners and the AAR community. It is a fantastic bonding experience. For the next few weeks, we are thrilled to use our new-harvest oil on the RSFP menus, grilling bread in the dining room's fireplace to make bruschette, and dousing them with olive oil for a heavenly antipasto.

The flavor of freshly pressed olive oil is really mind-blowing. It is full of flavonoids, which often give the oil a bright flavor, with an intense spectrum of pronounced herby, grassy, fruity, and spicy notes. With time, these small solids suspended in the oil settle at the bottom of the container, along with minute amounts of water. This sediment and water contribute over time to make the oil rancid. This is one reason olive oil has a shelf life of about a year, fortunately lasting until the following year's harvest.

New-harvest olive oil is also very special because it represents a time when people come together to help each other out and secure one of the principal ingredients, if not *the* principal ingredient, in their diet for the coming year.

CRUDO DI FINOCCHIO CON LIMONE, PREZZEMOLO E SCAGLIE DI PARMIGIANO

SHAVED FENNEL WITH LEMON JUICE, PARSLEY & PARMESAN

This is an instant favorite of anyone who tries it. It exemplifies the beauty of simplicity, and lets the ingredients speak for themselves. To make this dish shine, use the trick I learned from Russell Moore when I worked at Chez Panisse: shave the fennel thinly and dress it on the plate, not beforehand in a bowl. This detail is key, because it keeps every bite and each flavor distinct. I like to shave the Parmigiano using a vegetable peeler. Don't throw away the tough outer layer of the fennel bulbs; they can be roasted or braised (pp. 103, 115).

2 large fennel bulbs, trimmed

Freshly ground
black pepper, to taste

1 lemon

¼ cup (59 ml) new-harvest
extra virgin olive oil

12 parsley sprigs, leaves removed

1 oz (28 g) Grana Padano or
Parmigiano-Reggiano,
shaved with a peeler

Cut the fennel in half lengthwise and remove the tough outer layer. Soak the fennel in lots of water for 30 minutes to remove any dirt lodged within.

Shave the fennel as thinly as possible, either with a knife or, ideally, with a mandoline. Spread the fennel out on a platter. Season with salt and pepper.

Squeeze the juice of the lemon evenly over the fennel, from top to bottom and left to right.

Drizzle the olive oil over the fennel in the same way.

Garnish with the parsley leaves and the Parmigiano shavings. Serve immediately.

RAPE BIANCHE CON OLIO NUOVO

BOILED TURNIPS WITH NEW-HARVEST OLIVE OIL

One November, during a week of celebratory menus based around new-harvest olive oil, I remember working on the line in the Chez Panisse Café and preparing a plate of turnips that was sent to Alice Waters. Later, she came up to me and said, "You know, you can never undercook a turnip." That was her delicate way of telling me that I had overcooked them. Hot turnips continue to cook even after they are drained so keep this in mind. I love serving turnip greens with the turnips themselves if the greens look nice and vibrant.

8 medium turnips with stems and leaves (about 2 lbs [907 kg])

¼ cup (59 ml) new-harvest extra virgin olive oil

Bring a large pot of cold water to a boil.

Cut off the turnip stems leaving ¼ inch of stem attached to the turnip. Strip the leaves from the stems and wash them. Discard the stems. Peel the turnips if the skin is thick, cut them into wedges, and soak them in water for 30 minutes. Make sure you soak the turnip wedges in lots of water to get rid of any dirt lodged in the base of the green stem.

When the water comes to a rolling boil, salt it, and add the turnips and the turnip greens. Cook for 3 or 4 minutes, or until the turnips are just tender.

Drain the turnips and turnip greens and transfer them to a large bowl. Add some of the olive oil, season with salt, and toss well. Taste and adjust the seasoning with more salt and olive oil as necessary and serve immediately.

BRUSCHETTE CON FAGIOLI CANNELLINI, CAVOLO NERO E OLIO NUOVO

WHITE BEAN TOASTS WITH TUSCAN KALE
& NEW-HARVEST OLIVE OIL

———

One of the best things that one can experience in Italy is a good bruschetta, simply grilled over a wood fire, rubbed with garlic, and then doused with freshly pressed extra virgin olive oil. Every year, the Fellows, staff, and RSFP interns gather to pick the olives from the trees in the Bass Garden. The olives are pressed that same day in a local frantoio, or mill, that is owned by the families of two employees of the Academy, Paolo Imperatori and Mauro Abbatelli. With our new-harvest olive oil in hand, we like to start the week off with a selection of different bruschette. What makes these bruschette really special is the specific combination of flavors: the neutral creaminess of the beans along with the green cabbage flavor of the cavolo nero pair wonderfully with a healthy drizzle of the vibrant, spicy, bold flavor of new-harvest olive oil.

½ lb (227 g) cavolo nero or Lacinato, Tuscan, or dinosaur kale, leaves stripped from the stems

6 slices day-old rustic country bread, cut into ½-inch (1.3-cm)-thick slices

½ cup (118 ml) new-harvest extra virgin olive oil

1 garlic clove, peeled and cut in half

2 cups cooked cannellini beans (p. 219)

Preheat the oven to 400°F (204°C).

Bring a large pot of cold water to a boil.

When the water comes to a rolling boil, salt it, and blanch the kale for 4 minutes, or until the leaves are tender. Drain it and scatter the kale on a baking sheet to cool.

When the kale is cool enough to handle, squeeze out any remaining water and chop it.

Put the slices of bread on a baking sheet and toast them in the oven for about 10 minutes, flipping the toasts after 6 minutes, until the outside is crunchy on both sides but the inside is still soft and chewy.

Rub the toasts on one side with the garlic halves and drizzle or brush with a little olive oil.

In a large bowl, combine the beans (make sure they are drained well) and kale and toss them with ¼ cup olive oil. Taste and adjust the seasoning. Carefully arrange the beans and kale on top of the toast and drizzle with the remaining new-harvest olive oil. Serve immediately.

BROCCOLO ROMANESCO LESSO CON OLIO NUOVO E LIMONE
LONG-COOKED ROMANESCO BROCCOLI
WITH NEW-HARVEST OLIVE OIL & LEMON

Italians love their vegetables cooked for a long time, and by most American standards, they might be considered greatly overcooked. After living in Italy for an extended period of time, though, I have come to realize that the flavor spectrum and texture of vegetables change tremendously the more vegetables cook, often even improving.

I now love long-cooked vegetables, and Romanesco broccoli is probably my favorite. It has an amazing texture, and, unlike broccoli or cauliflower, it holds its shape as it cooks, even to the point when it is so soft that you can mash it with a fork. This preparation is very special in the late fall, when extra virgin olive oil has just been pressed. The new-harvest olive oil is vibrant and green (amazingly, some oils appear almost fluorescent) and the Romanesco is the ideal vehicle to showcase the oil's bold flavors.

1 head Romanesco broccoli (about 2 lbs [907 g]), trimmed and cut into equal-sized florets

3 tablespoons new-harvest extra virgin olive oil

1 lemon

Bring a large pot of cold water to a boil.

When the water comes to a rolling boil, salt it, and add the Romanesco. Cook, stirring occasionally, for about 10 minutes, or until it is very soft. Drain the Romanesco and transfer it to a medium bowl. Toss with olive oil, the juice of ½ a lemon, and season with salt. Taste and adjust the seasoning with more lemon juice and salt as needed. Serve immediately.

INVERNO

INVERNO
WINTER

Even in sunny, temperate Rome, winter often feels like the longest season of the year. When the Fellows arrive at the Academy in the fall, I doubt they realize that those first broccoli and cabbages in the fall are what they will be eating for the next five months. I often find that in winter people struggle the most to maintain a seasonal diet. Think about not eating a fresh tomato for more than seven months, from November to June: it isn't easy.

That said, even though the sweet fruits and vegetables of summer are a distant memory, and fall fruits are fading, winter actually has a fantastic repertoire of fruits and vegetables. There are artichokes, citrus, root vegetables, winter squashes, cabbages, different broccoli, chicories, and bitter greens, as well as the potatoes, onions, and garlic that are cured for dry storage, and, of course, jarred tomatoes. Not bad. Not to mention how delicious the rich, comforting, sweet, and bitter foods of winter can be.

One of the most fascinating things about winter is that unlike during all the other seasons, nearly all vegetables get sweeter as the season progresses, peaking in sweetness when the weather is coldest. Contrasting with this sweetness are the bitter greens that Romans love to eat during the winter. At the Academy, we do, too. In fact, one of the most iconic dishes, bitter greens *ripassati* (sautéed with garlic and hot pepper flakes), is a favorite of the AAR community. We serve bitter greens, prepared in many different ways, at just about every meal.

Italians often blanch or flash-boil vegetables before sautéing or cooking them, to remove bitterness or to round out strong flavors. Blanching the vegetables first also lightens heavier preparations (like gratins, braises, or stews) and facilitates cooking by softening the fibers of the vegetable. I think that this blanching trick is one of the most helpful little secrets of Italian cuisine; it ensures that the secondary cooking technique or preparation will be lighter and more delicate.

CARCIOFI ALLA ROMANA
ROMAN-STYLE ARTICHOKES

This is the RSFP's version of the Roman classic. Traditionally these artichokes are stuffed with a little chopped garlic and a wild variety of mint known as mentuccia, but I prefer to smash the garlic and use whole mint sprigs mixed in among the artichokes because it lends a more delicate perfume. I also like to let the artichokes fry a little, slowly, until they are golden brown on the bottom, which is not traditional but makes for a stunning presentation. The frying can only happen once the artichokes have become completely tender and the lid has been removed so that excess moisture can evaporate.

1 lemon (for cleaning the artichokes)

6 globe artichokes, cleaned (p. 225), and lemon water reserved

½ cup (118 ml) extra virgin olive oil

6 garlic cloves, peeled and smashed

8 mint sprigs

Season the artichokes with salt and place them upside down in a high-sided pot so that the stem is sticking up. Add the olive oil and let the artichokes sit for 10 minutes to allow the salt to be absorbed.

Scatter the garlic and mint over the artichokes, and pour in enough of the reserved lemon water to come about ¼ inch (.6 cm) up the sides of the pot. Cover the pot with a lid and turn the heat to medium-low. Cook, rotating the pot to allow even cooking, until a paring knife easily penetrates the thickest part of the base of the artichoke. Turn the heat to low, remove the lid, and allow the artichokes to start browning, rotating the pot over the heat for even browning. When the artichokes have browned on the bottom, remove them from the heat and serve immediately or at room temperature.

CARCIOFI FRITTI
FRIED ARTICHOKES

We often serve these artichokes for lunch since they retain their crispiness for a long time after they are fried, which is always difficult to pull off with fried food. They are also phenomenal as snacks or as an appetizer. Cleaning artichokes is a labor-intensive process, and artichokes are expensive, but serving them this way—as slices, rather than as whole artichokes—yields more servings per artichoke. The end result should be like little artichoke chips—thin, light, and wonderfully crispy.

4 globe artichokes, cleaned (p. 225)

2 lemons (one for the lemon water and one cut into wedges)

2 quarts (1.9 l) vegetable oil

9 oz (255 g) all-purpose flour

Remove the artichoke from the lemon water and cut it in half lengthwise. Scoop out the choke (fuzzy part of the heart) using a small spoon. Dip the artichoke in the lemon water once again and return it to the board.

Slice the artichokes thinly with a knife or using a mandoline, and immediately return the slices to the lemon water.

Put the vegetable oil in a high-sided pot over medium heat. Make sure the oil does not go more than halfway up the sides of the pot.

When the oil has reached 350°F (177°C), drain the artichoke slices and pat them dry with a kitchen towel. Put the flour in a large bowl, add the artichokes, and toss well. Carefully lower the artichokes into the oil using a slotted spoon and fry them in small batches, until golden, repeating as necessary and making sure that the temperature of the oil is consistently at 350°F (177°C). Remove the artichokes using a slotted spoon and place them on paper towels to drain. Sprinkle with salt and serve with lemon wedges.

INSALATA DI SCAROLA CON CARDI, ACCIUGHE E CROSTINI DI PANE

ESCAROLE CAESAR SALAD

WITH CARDOONS, ANCHOVIES & CROUTONS

The true origins of Caesar salad are debatable, but everyone seems to agree that it was invented by an Italian-American during Prohibition, which is one of the many reasons we love to eat this salad at an American institution in Italy! Caesar salad is an RSFP favorite, and the amazing crunchiness and sweetness that escarole provides is particularly satisfying. Our former sous-chef Giovanni Guerrera used to make a great version of Caesar salad with Tuscan kale instead of escarole. Cardoons and croutons also add great texture to this salad, and the cardoons add a slight bitterness as well. However, the labor-intensive cardoons are purely optional here.

1 batch croutons (p. 203)

1 batch aïoli (p. 201)

8 whole salt-packed anchovies, cleaned (p. 223) or 16 tinned anchovy fillets in oil

1 garlic clove, peeled

1½ oz (43 g) Parmigiano-Reggiano, grated (about ½ cup), plus more to taste

Freshly ground black pepper, to taste

1 to 2 lemons

1 small bunch cardoons, cleaned (p. 79), blanched, and cut into ½-inch (1.3-cm) pieces, optional

2 heads escarole inner leaves, trimmed and cut into ½-inch (1.3-cm) ribbons

Pound the anchovies in a mortar and pestle until you obtain a paste. Remove and set them aside. In the same mortar and pestle pound the garlic until you obtain a paste. If you don't have a mortar and pestle, finely chop the anchovies and garlic.

Add the garlic, anchovies, and Parmigiano to the aïoli and adjust the seasoning with salt, pepper, and some freshly squeezed lemon juice. Let sit for 30 minutes so that the flavors can develop.

In a medium bowl, toss the croutons and cardoons (if you're using them) with ½ cup of the anchovy dressing. In a large bowl, lightly season the escarole with salt, pepper, and lemon juice. Add the remaining dressing, toss well, and add the croutons and cardoons. Taste and adjust the seasoning. Serve immediately with more pepper and Parmigiano, if you like.

CARDI IN UMIDO ALLA CIOCIARA
CARDOONS STEWED IN TOMATO SAUCE WITH MARJORAM

Cardoons are members of the thistle family, closely related to artichokes and very similar in appearance to the artichoke plant. We learned this recipe from Oretta Zanini De Vita's book The Food of Rome and Lazio, *the RSFP bible. This preparation is reminiscent of the way in which cardoons are prepared in the Ciociaria region of Lazio, the countryside south of Rome. This dish is traditionally made with mentuccia, but a combination of marjoram and parsley works well.*

1 lemon (for the lemon water)

1 bunch of cardoons (about 2 lbs [907 g]), trimmed

⅓ cup (79 ml) extra virgin olive oil

3 garlic cloves, peeled and smashed

6 marjoram sprigs, picked and chopped (about 1 tablespoon)

10 parsley sprigs, picked and chopped (about 3 tablespoons)

1 teaspoon hot pepper flakes

56 oz (1.6 kg) canned whole San Marzano-style tomatoes, pureed with a hand blender or in a food processor

Fill a large bowl with 1 gallon (3.8 l) of water and add the juice of 1 lemon (add the lemon halves as well) to prevent the cardoons from turning brown. Using a paring knife or vegetable peeler peel away the fibrous rib running along the backside of the cardoon stalks. With a clean kitchen towel rub away any soft white fuzz off the underside and inner stalks. Cut away the spiky sides of the cardoon ribs and immediately place the cardoons in the lemon water.

Bring a large pot of cold water to a boil then salt it, drain the cardoons and add them to the boiling water. Cook for 12 to 15 minutes, or until tender. Drain them and scatter on a baking sheet to cool. Slice the cardoons diagonally about ½-inch (1.3-cm)-thick.

Put the olive oil and garlic in a 14-inch (36-cm) sauté pan and gently fry the garlic until it is golden, then remove and discard it. Add the herbs and hot pepper flakes and sizzle for 15 seconds. Immediately add the tomato puree, bring to a simmer, and cook over medium heat for 12 minutes. Add the cardoons and simmer for about 20 minutes. Taste and adjust seasoning; serve immediately.

BROCCOLETTI RIPASSATI IN PADELLA
BROCCOLI RABE SAUTÉED WITH GARLIC & HOT PEPPER

———

Romans love just about any greens ripassati in padella *(sautéed with olive oil, garlic, and hot pepper flakes). Broccoli napoletani are one of those strange Old World vegetables that few people ever have heard of, let alone seen. Giovanni Bernabei, one of our farmers, introduced us to broccoli napoletani a few winters ago when he came across some seeds and decided to plant them. Giovanni brought us a plant to put in the Bass Garden, which we let go to seed, and we can now plant it in abundance. This vegetable is in the broccoli family, and its leaves look like the leaves of the broccoli (which, by the way, are edible and delicious), but they have the texture of Tuscan kale. If you can't find broccoli napoletani, we recommend using the leaves of the broccoli plant or the more prevalent and more bitter broccoli rabe (broccoletti in Italian) as a substitute. Beet greens, dandelion greens, or any other bitter greens also work well here.*

---

2 lbs (907 g) broccoli rabe, broccoli leaves, or broccoli napoletani, trimmed

½ cup (118 ml) extra virgin olive oil

4 garlic cloves, peeled and smashed

2 teaspoons hot pepper flakes

Bring a large pot of cold water to a boil.

When the water comes to a rolling boil, salt it and add the broccoli rabe. Cook for about 6 minutes, or until tender. Drain the broccoli rabe and scatter the leaves on a baking sheet to cool.

When the broccoli rabe is cool enough to handle, gently squeeze out some of the remaining water (if you use broccoli leaves, roughly chop them).

Put the garlic and olive oil in a 12-inch (30-cm) sauté pan over medium-low heat and gently fry the garlic, stirring occasionally, until it is golden. Add the hot pepper and sizzle for 30 seconds. Add the broccoli rabe and sauté for a few more minutes, mixing well until the flavors have combined. Taste and adjust the seasoning and serve immediately or at room temperature.

PUNTARELLE IN SALSA DI ALICI
CATALAN CHICORY WITH ANCHOVY VINAIGRETTE

———

This classic Roman contorno is an absolute must if you're ever in Rome in the winter. Puntarelle are a member of the chicory family, and their leaves look like dandelion greens (if the dandelion plant is left to go to seed, it very closely resembles a puntarelle plant). We use a special tool shown on the opposite page that slices the shoots into a julienne. These slices are then placed in ice water for a few hours until they start to curl up into tight balls and become crisp. At the RSFP we sometimes add blanched cardoons and homemade croutons to make a "sort of Caesar" salad.

1 garlic clove, peeled

½ cup (118 ml) extra virgin olive oil

6 salt-packed anchovies, cleaned (p. 223) or 12 tinned anchovy fillets in oil

¼ cup (59 ml) red wine vinegar

2 lbs (907 g) puntarelle or dandelion greens, trimmed

Freshly ground black pepper, to taste

Pound the garlic in a mortar and pestle or finely chop it. Remove and set it aside with a few drops of olive oil. Pound the anchovies in the mortar and pestle or finely chop them. Combine the anchovies, garlic, red wine vinegar, and olive oil in a small bowl and whisk well. Let sit for 1 hour to allow the flavors to develop.

Push the thick white (usually hollow) stems of the puntarelle through the cutter, or cut each stem lengthwise into very thin strips. If you are using dandelion greens, simply trim them and cut them into bite-sized pieces. Transfer the cut puntarelle to a bowl of ice water, adding the green leaves as well if you like. Soak them for at least 1 hour. Drain and dry them well using a salad spinner.

Transfer the puntarelle to a large bowl and season lightly with salt and pepper. Dress with the anchovy vinaigrette and toss well to combine. Let the dressed puntarelle sit for a few minutes to allow the flavors to develop. Taste and adjust the seasoning, and serve.

MISTO OFFICINALIS DI ERBE SPONTANEE DI GIOVANNI BERNABEI CON PATATE

GIOVANNI BERNABEI'S MISTICANZA WITH POTATOES

Giovanni Bernabei's misto is a mix of herbs and wild greens foraged from his land and the surrounding mountainside. Giovanni also grows the most amazing potatoes I have ever had. Part of his philosophy is to dry farm: if it rains, there is water for the crops, and if it doesn't, there isn't. This forces the plant to compete for its nutrients making it much heartier and producing more flavorful potatoes. We like to add red onions to the potatoes for sweetness if the greens are very bitter.

2 lbs (907 g) misticanza, or other mixed bitter greens, such as dandelion greens, broccoli rabe, and escarole outers, trimmed

2 lbs (907 g) Yukon gold potatoes, peeled and cut into 1-inch (2.5-cm) dice (keep in cold water until needed)

⅔ cup (158 ml) extra virgin olive oil

4 garlic cloves, peeled and smashed

2 teaspoons hot pepper flakes

Bring a large pot of cold water to a boil, then salt it and blanch the greens for about 4 minutes, or until tender. Remove them using a slotted spoon (reserve the water for the potatoes), and scatter on a baking sheet to cool.

Add the potatoes to the reserved boiling water and blanch them for about 12 minutes, or until tender. They should fall apart when smashed with a fork. Drain them and scatter on a baking sheet to cool.

When the potatoes are cool, put ½ cup olive oil in a 14-inch (36-cm) sauté pan over medium heat and add the potatoes. Gently fry the potatoes until they start to crisp up and turn golden. Add the garlic and hot pepper and continue frying for 3 minutes. If the garlic starts to brown, remove and discard it.

When the greens are cool enough to handle, squeeze out most of the excess water. Add the misticanza to the potatoes and add the remaining oil if the pan looks dry. Continue to sauté for 5 minutes or until the flavors are well combined. Taste and adjust the seasoning, and serve immediately.

CAVOLFIORE ALLA ROMANA
ROMAN-STYLE CAULIFLOWER

I distinctly remember this dish as one of my most profound culinary revelations. When I worked at Stars in San Francisco, Morgan Brownlow, an extremely gifted cook and a friend, prepared this dish one afternoon. I had a habit of getting to work a little ahead of my shift, because I liked to poke around the kitchen and ask Morgan questions about how he was preparing things. One day, he lifted the lid of the pot in which he was cooking Cavolfiore alla Romana, and it changed everything for me. I used to hate cauliflower; I found it tasted too strongly of cabbage, but here the cauliflower was long-cooked, sweet and tender—I instantly loved it. The powerful soffritto of anchovies, garlic, and rosemary completely disguised the strong cabbage smell that had always bothered me when I was a child. This dish was a real game-changer for me, and if you aren't a fan of cauliflower, I hope it will be for you as well. It is fantastic with roasted lamb.

1 large head cauliflower or Romanesco broccoli (about 2 lbs [907 g]), cut into florets

⅔ cup (158 ml) extra virgin olive oil

3 garlic cloves, peeled and chopped

1 teaspoon hot pepper flakes

1 large rosemary sprig, picked and chopped

4 salt-packed anchovies, cleaned (p. 223), or 8 tinned anchovy fillets in oil

½ lemon, optional

Bring a large pot of cold water to a boil.

When the water comes to a rolling boil, salt it, and blanch the cauliflower for 3 minutes, or until just tender, and drain it.

Put the olive oil and garlic in a 14-inch (36-cm) high-sided sauté pan over medium-low heat and cook, stirring occasionally, until the garlic is just golden. Add the hot pepper flakes, chopped rosemary, and anchovies, and sizzle for 30 seconds, or until the anchovies have started to melt into the oil. Immediately add the cauliflower and stir well. Cover the pan with a lid and stew the cauliflower for about 20 minutes, stirring occasionally, until it is coated with the anchovy oil and has become meltingly tender. Add a little water to the pan if the cauliflower starts to stick or brown. You should be able to mash it with a fork. Taste and adjust the seasoning and add some lemon juice if you like a bit of acidity. Serve immediately.

ZUCCA IN SAOR
BUTTERNUT SQUASH IN SWEET & SOUR SAUCE

The first time I made this was with James Ehrlich, an intern at the RSFP in the summer and fall of 2011. He discovered this recipe in one of our cookbooks, and decided to make it for the meal that each intern creates and executes at the end of the internship. We loved James's choice of zucca in saor so much that we made a few modifications to the original recipe to come up with our own version here at the RSFP. Saor is traditionally a Venetian preparation for fish; it is similar to scapece, because it usually consists of something fried and then marinated, often in a sweet and sour mixture.

¼ cup raisins

1 cup (237 ml) white wine

6 tablespoons white wine vinegar

1 butternut squash (about 3 lbs [1.4 kg]) peeled, seeded, and cut into 1-inch (2.5-cm) dice

1 cup (237 ml) extra virgin olive oil

2 large yellow onions, peeled and thinly sliced

3 whole cloves

3 bay leaves

¼ cup pine nuts

4.5 oz (128 g) all-purpose flour

Preheat the oven to 300°F (149°C).

Put the raisins, wine, and vinegar in a small saucepan over medium heat. Bring to a boil and turn off the heat. Set the pot aside and let the raisins plump in the liquid for 20 minutes.

Season the squash with salt and let it sit for 15 minutes.

Put ¼ cup of the olive oil, the onions, cloves, bay leaves, and a pinch of salt in a 10-inch (25-cm) sauté pan over medium heat. Add a pinch of salt and cook, stirring occasionally, until the onions are translucent. Make sure the onions don't brown. Remove the pan from the heat and set aside.

Toast the pine nuts in the oven on a rimmed baking sheet for about 7 minutes, or until they are fragrant and just lightly golden.

In a large bowl, toss the squash with the flour. Put the remaining ¾ cup olive oil in a 14-inch (36-cm) sauté pan over medium heat. When the oil is hot, add the squash and gently fry it on all sides (work in batches if necessary).

When the squash is fried, discard any excess olive oil in the pan and add the cooked onions along with the liquid from the raisins, reserving the raisins for later. Turn the heat to medium high and let the squash simmer in the onions for 10 minutes. Remove the bay leaf, taste and adjust the seasoning, top with raisins and pine nuts, and serve at room temperature.

BRUSCHETTE DI BROCCOLI E 'NDUJA
BROCCOLI & 'NDUJA TOASTS

'Nduja (pronounced in-doo-ya) is a really delicious, very spicy Calabrian sausage that is made with fermented hot chilis and a very high percentage of fat. It is so soft that it can be spread on bread or pizza. 'Nduja is fantastic simply melted and tossed with long-cooked broccoli. If you can't find 'nduja in stores, try making it from scratch (p. 214).

4 tablespoons 'nduja
(to make your own see p. 214)

1 head broccoli
(about 1 lb [454 g]),
cut into florets

¼ cup (59 ml) extra virgin
olive oil, plus 2 tablespoons

1 medium red onion,
peeled and thinly sliced

1 garlic clove,
peeled and cut in half

6 slices day-old
rustic country bread, cut into
½-inch (1.3-cm)-thick slices

Preheat the oven to 400°F (204°C).

Bring a large pot of cold water to a boil.

When the water comes to a rolling boil, salt it and blanch the broccoli for 2 or 3 minutes, until it is barely tender. Remove it using a slotted spoon and reserve the broccoli water.

Put the olive oil, onions, and a pinch of salt in a 14-inch (36-cm) sauté pan over medium-low heat. Cook, stirring occasionally, until the onions are translucent. Add the broccoli and stir well, then add ½ cup (118 ml) of the reserved broccoli water. Cover the pan with a lid and stew the broccoli until it is very tender, about 15 minutes, adding broccoli water as necessary. When the broccoli is meltingly tender and most of the water has evaporated, add the 'nduja and mix well. Turn off the heat and taste and adjust the seasoning.

Put the slices of bread on a baking sheet, brush on both sides with olive oil and toast for about 10 minutes, flipping the slices after 6 minutes, until crunchy outside but still soft inside.

Rub the toasts with half of a garlic clove when the bread is still warm. Spoon the broccoli and 'nduja mixture over the toasts and serve immediately.

CICORIA ALL'AGRO

DANDELION GREENS WITH LEMON & OLIVE OIL

This is one of my absolute favorite vegetable dishes in Roman cuisine. In many trattorie dandelion greens are prepared ripassati, sautéed with garlic and hot pepper, but I prefer them prepared in this simple way. The combination of lemon juice and olive oil perfectly complements the bitterness of the greens. The key here is to squeeze the water out of the cooked greens, but to not squeeze them completely dry. Leaving a little water in the greens dilutes the acidity of the lemon juice, requires less olive oil, and creates a balanced, light, lemony, juicy dish.

2 lbs (907 g) dandelion greens or cicoria, trimmed

2 lemons

⅓ cup (79 ml) extra virgin olive oil

Bring a large pot of cold water to a boil.

When the water comes to a rolling boil, salt it, and add the greens. Cook for about 6 minutes, or until they are completely tender. Drain the dandelion greens and scatter them on a baking sheet to cool.

When the greens are cool enough to handle, squeeze them gently with your hands to get rid of some of the excess water. Transfer the dandelion greens to a bowl and add the juice of 1 lemon and some of the olive oil. Adjust the seasoning with salt and add more lemon juice or olive oil as necessary. Serve immediately.

VERZA ROSSA ALLE MELE
GIO'S RED CABBAGE & APPLES

We always have trouble using up all the red cabbage brought to us by our farmers. While cabbage is often better suited to raw preparations, Giovanni Guerrera showed us this recipe for cooked cabbage one winter and I remember loving its distinct balance and apple flavor. This is maybe the best cabbage and apple recipe I have ever tried, and it is a perfect German-inspired accompaniment to braised or roasted pork. This dish can also be prepared a day or two in advance to let the flavors develop; I actually think it gets better with a little time to set. It is also delicious served cold or at room temperature. It is important to use good apple juice that isn't too sweet and has good acidity.

4 tablespoons (57 g) butter

1 medium yellow onion, peeled and thinly sliced

4 medium Goldrush or Granny Smith apples, cored and thinly sliced

1 head red cabbage (about 3 lbs [1.4 kg]) cored and thinly sliced

2 cups (473 ml) organic apple juice, no sugar added

⅓ cup (79 ml) apple cider vinegar

Put the butter, onions, and apples in a high-sided pot over medium-low heat and cook, stirring frequently, for about 15 minutes, or until the apples are soft and the onions are translucent.

Add the cabbage and apple juice, mix well, and cover with a lid. Cook over medium-low heat for about 45 minutes, stirring every 15 minutes and adding a little water as the liquid reduces so that the cabbage braises in liquid.

When the cabbage is tender and the liquid has evaporated, add the apple cider vinegar and adjust the seasoning with salt. Serve warm or at room temperature.

BIETA GRATINATA
CHARD GRATIN
––––––––

Every time I make a gratin, I think of Pellegrino Artusi, the renowned Italian cookbook author famous for his The Science of Cooking and the Art of Eating Well, *published in 1891. This cookbook was one of the first to discuss the famous scientific method of trial and error and apply it to cooking. I agree with Artusi when he says that almost all winter vegetables are divine when mixed with besciamella and gratinéed in the oven, but I am partial to chard. A key ingredient here is Parmigiano-Reggiano, because its sharpness helps cut through the richness of the besciamella. This dish is particularly good on a cold winter night when you need something hearty that sticks to your ribs.*

2 cups homemade breadcrumbs (p. 205)

1 batch besciamella (p. 215)

1½ bunches chard

2 oz (57 g) Parmigiano-Reggiano (about ¾ cup grated)

Freshly ground black pepper, to taste

1 tablespoon (14 g) butter

Preheat the oven to 375°F (190°C).

Bring a large pot of cold water to a boil.

Strip the chard leaves from the stems. Cut the stems diagonally, roughly ¼-inch (.6-cm)-thick. When the water comes to a rolling boil, salt it, and add the stems. Cook for 5 minutes, then add the chard leaves and cook for 3 or 4 more minutes, or until both the leaves and stems are tender. Remove everything using a slotted spoon and scatter on a baking sheet to cool.

When the chard is cool enough to handle, gently squeeze out any excess water. In a large bowl, combine the chard leaves, stems, besciamella, and ½ cup of the Parmigiano. Taste and adjust the seasoning with salt and pepper. Put half of the breadcrumbs in a food processor and pulse until finely ground. Butter a medium rectangular baking dish and cover with the finely ground breadcrumbs. Transfer the chard mixture to the baking dish and bake for 25 minutes, or until golden brown. Top with remaining Parmigiano and coarse breadcrumbs right after it comes out of the oven. Let sit for 10 minutes and serve hot.

FRITTELLE DI BORRAGINE

BORAGE FRITTERS WITH ANCHOVIES & PECORINO ROMANO

Borage is a wild green with a leaf that looks almost thistle-like. When cooked, the prickly spines of the leaves soften and become unnoticeable. The inspiration for this recipe comes from Giovanni Bernabei's wife, Assunta. She likes to put an anchovy fillet in between two borage leaves and dip this little package into a pastella (frying batter). Domenico Cortese, a cook at the RSFP for more than three years, is definitely the "fry king" in the Academy kitchen, and he adapted Assunta's recipe to make these borage fritters.

1 lb (454 g) borage, leaves stripped from stems

¼ cup (59 ml) plus 1 tablespoon extra virgin olive oil

3 garlic cloves, peeled and smashed

1 teaspoon hot pepper flakes

17 oz (503 ml) lukewarm water

.35 oz (10 g) brewer's yeast

1 lb (454 g) all-purpose flour

2 egg yolks

3 oz (85 g) pecorino Romano (about ¾ cup)

4 salt-packed anchovies, cleaned and chopped (p. 223) or 8 tinned anchovy fillets in oil, chopped

4 quarts (3.8 l) vegetable oil

Bring a large pot of cold water to a boil.

When the water comes to a rolling boil, salt it, and add the borage leaves. Cook for about 5 minutes, or until very tender. Drain the borage and scatter it on a baking sheet to cool. When the borage is cool enough to handle, squeeze out any remaining water and chop it.

Put ¼ cup olive oil and the garlic in a 14-inch (36-cm) sauté pan over medium-low heat. Cook, stirring occasionally, until the garlic is golden, then remove and discard it. Immediately add the hot pepper and the borage and sauté until the borage is coated in oil. Season with salt and turn off the heat.

Pour the lukewarm water into a large bowl. Add the yeast and mix well. Add a large pinch of salt and 1 tablespoon olive oil. Gradually add the flour, mixing constantly, until you obtain a thick batter. Stir in the egg yolks, borage, pecorino, and chopped anchovies. Cover the bowl with plastic wrap and let sit for 1½ to 2 hours, until the mixture has doubled in volume.

Pour the vegetable oil into a medium high-sided pot over medium heat. Make sure the oil does not come more than halfway up the sides of the pot. When the oil reaches 385°F (196°C), use a tablespoon to scoop the batter and carefully lower it into the oil. Fry until golden brown on both sides, about 2 minutes per side. Remove the borage fritters from the oil with a slotted spoon and drain them on paper towels. Sprinkle with salt and serve immediately.

CRUDO DI FINOCCHIO AGLI AGRUMI

SHAVED FENNEL WITH CITRUS

This is our California-inspired twist on the classic Italian dish of fennel and oranges. I prefer to use a mix of citrus here, and you should feel free to experiment with your favorites. True to my Californian roots, I like to dress the shaved fennel with a delicious vinaigrette made with macerated onions and lots of citrus zest and juice. This is a perfect winter dish because citrus fruits peak in cold weather: when the temperature drops, the tree uses all of its energy to preserve and extend the life of the fruit, which makes it sweeter.

2 large fennel bulbs, trimmed

2 medium shallots, peeled and minced

1 lemon, zested with a grater or microplane and juiced

1 orange, zested with a grater or microplane, peeled, and sliced (p. 231)

1 pink grapefruit zested with a grater or microplane, peeled, and sliced (p. 231)

3 tablespoons freshly squeezed orange juice

3 tablespoons freshly squeezed grapefruit juice

3 tablespoons white wine vinegar

¼ cup (59 ml) extra virgin olive oil

Freshly ground black pepper, to taste

12 parsley sprigs, leaves removed

Cut the fennel in half lengthwise and remove the tough outer layer. Soak the fennel in lots of water for 30 minutes to remove any dirt lodged between the layers.

Combine the shallots, citrus zest, citrus juice, and vinegar in a small bowl. Season with salt and let macerate for at least 1 hour.

Arrange the citrus slices on a platter. Shave the fennel as thinly as possible, either with a knife or with a mandoline. Carefully spread the fennel evenly over the citrus and season with salt and pepper.

Add the olive oil to the dressing and whisk well until the vinaigrette has emulsified, taste, and adjust the seasoning with salt and pepper. Spoon the vinaigrette over the fennel and citrus salad. Garnish with the parsley leaves and serve immediately.

AL FORNO
BROASTING & ROASTING

Roasting is a cooking technique that relies on dry heat—from a flame, an oven, or another heat source. At the RSFP, we like to roast everything "slow and low," meaning that we prefer to roast in the oven at a lower temperature and for a longer amount of time than is traditional. When roasting vegetables, this process allows for their natural sweetness to develop as they cook and ensures a wonderful caramelization. Perfectly roasted vegetables are soft and creamy on the inside and beautifully browned on the outside.

Braising is called a combination cooking technique, because it uses dry heat as well as moist heat. When braising, the food is seared or browned first, put in a high-sided pot or casserole dish, and then covered one third of the way up the side of the vessel with some kind of liquid (water, wine, or broth). The pot or dish is then covered with a lid, and the contents cook slowly over low heat on a stovetop or in the oven until tender. The steam from the cooking juices is a very powerful tenderizer. This is a method often used on meat.

"Broasting" isn't an official cooking technique, but is a combination of roasting and braising that I learned at Chez Panisse, where we would broast almost anything. Broasting, like braising, uses both dry and moist heat, but when broasting, the food is braised first and then roasted or browned after, instead of vice versa. We use this technique all the time at the RSFP. Vegetables or meat are put in a covered baking dish with a tiny bit of water and olive oil that create steam during the cooking process. Once the vegetables are tender, we uncover the baking dish and roast until the vegetable juice in the pan has evaporated and the meat or vegetables are a gorgeous golden brown color.

RAPE INVERNALI AL FORNO CON SALVIA
ROASTED ROOT VEGETABLES WITH SAGE

———

In my opinion the key to deliciously sweet caramelized roasted root vegetables lies in their preparation: slow roasting is the only way to go. Roasting at a low temperature for a long period of time brings out the candy-like sweetness of root vegetables, which is marvelously complemented by the resinous sage leaves, while roasting at a higher temperature can create a leathery skin and unpleasant texture. I like to roast the different root vegetables separately to ensure that they cook evenly and maintain a distinct flavor, and I only combine them at the end.

½ butternut squash (about 1½ lbs [680 g]), peeled, seeded, and cut into ⅓-inch (.8-cm) cubes

1 celery root, peeled and cut into ½-inch (1.3-cm) tiles

10 tablespoons extra virgin olive oil

30 sage leaves

4 carrots, peeled and cut into ⅓-inch (.8-cm) coins

3 parsnips, peeled and cut into ⅓-inch (.8-cm) coins

2 red onions, peeled and cut into ⅓-inch (.8-cm) wedges

Preheat the oven to 300°F (149°C).

In a large bowl, toss the butternut squash and celery root with 5 tablespoons of the olive oil and 15 of the sage leaves; season with salt. Put them on a rimmed baking sheet lined with parchment paper.

In the same bowl, toss the carrots and parsnips with 3 tablespoons of the olive oil and 10 of the sage leaves; season with salt. Put them on a rimmed baking sheet lined with parchment paper.

Toss the red onions in the bowl with 2 tablespoon of the olive oil and 5 of the sage leaves; season with salt. Put them on a rimmed baking sheet lined with parchment paper.

Roast all three baking sheets of vegetables for about an hour, stirring every 15 to 20 minutes to ensure even cooking and caramelization. I often find that the onions are caramelized after about 1 hour, while the other root vegetables take a little longer. Combine all the vegetables and serve immediately or at room temperature.

FINOCCHIO IN UMIDO CON ALLORO E TIMO
BROASTED FENNEL WITH BAY LEAF & THYME

This recipe is an excellent way to showcase the broasting technique, combining braising, baking, and roasting. When the baked fennel is tender, it can continue to roast until it has browned and become caramelized, or it can be removed from the oven and grilled, gratinéed, or seared in a pan. Our version includes a fried herb salsa verde, which makes this fennel especially wonderful served with grilled fish and roasts.

1 batch salsa verde (p. 213)

3 fennel bulbs, trimmed and cut into ¼-inch (.6-cm) wedges

¼ cup (59 ml) extra virgin olive oil

8 thyme sprigs

3 bay leaves

6 cups (1.4 l) vegetable oil

8 sage sprigs, leaves removed (about 1 cup)

6 large rosemary sprigs, needles removed (about 1 cup)

Preheat the oven to 350°F (177°C).

Soak the fennel wedges in lots of water for 30 minutes to dislodge any dirt within.

In a large bowl, toss the fennel with the olive oil and season with salt. Transfer the fennel to a large rectangular baking dish. Add ⅓ cup water and scatter the thyme and bay leaves. Cover tightly with aluminum foil and bake for about 40 minutes, mixing every 20 minutes. When the fennel is tender, remove the foil and continue baking for 20 minutes until it is slightly browned and caramelized.

Put the vegetable oil in a small high-sided pot over medium heat. Make sure the oil does not come more than halfway up the sides of the pot. When the oil reaches 350°F (177°C), carefully lower the rosemary needles and fry them for about 45 seconds, or until the sizzling has reduced (this will happen very quickly) and the needles are crunchy. Quickly remove the needles using a slotted spoon and drain them on paper towels. Repeat this same process for the sage.

Crumble the fried herbs into the salsa verde and drizzle it over the fennel. Serve warm or at room temperature.

TOPINAMBUR AL FORNO
CON GREMOLATA DI ARANCE E NOCCIOLE

ROASTED SUNCHOKES

WITH ORANGE-HAZELNUT GREMOLATA

It is commonly believed that the name Jerusalem artichoke came from a mispronunciation of the plant's Italian family name girasole, or sunflower. Apparently, girasole was misinterpreted as Gerusalemme, or Jerusalem. A more probable explanation is that these tubers are called sunchokes because, just like the sunflower, the flower of the sunchoke plant rotates with the sun—thus their latin name, helianthus tuberosus, deriving from the ancient Greek word for sun, helios. Jerusalem artichokes or sunchokes are nice and sweet, especially when roasted (although they are also terrific served raw in salads). They have a pleasant spice-like quality, which is why I like to pair them with this gremolata made of toasted hazelnuts and orange zest that perfectly complements and brings forward their natural sweetness and spice.

3 lbs (1.4 kg) sunchokes, peeled and cut into ⅓-inch (1.3-cm) slices

⅓ cup (79 ml) extra virgin olive oil

1 orange

1 garlic clove, peeled

15 parsley sprigs, picked and chopped (about 4 tablespoons)

2 sage leaves

3 tablespoons toasted hazelnuts, finely chopped (p. 233)

Freshly ground black pepper, to taste

Preheat the oven to 375°F (190°C).

Toss the sunchoke slices with the olive oil and season with salt. Transfer them to a baking sheet lined with parchment paper or to a baking dish. Roast for about an hour until they are roasted and slightly caramelized, stirring them every 15 minutes to ensure even cooking and caramelization.

Make the gremolata: using a vegetable peeler, peel four or five strips of orange rind (about ½ the rind of the orange). Finely mince the garlic, parsley, sage leaves, and orange peel together. Add the finely chopped hazelnuts and season with salt and black pepper. As soon as the sunchokes come out of the oven, sprinkle the gremolata directly on top of the hot roasted sunchokes still on the baking sheet or in the baking dish, so that the gremolata sizzles in the excess oil in the pan. Taste and adjust the seasoning, and serve immediately.

RADICCHIO DI TREVISO AL FORNO CON CIPOLLE ROSSE E ACETO BALSAMICO

ROASTED TREVISO RADICCHIO
WITH RED ONIONS & BALSAMIC VINEGAR

There are many different kinds of radicchio, and they are often named after the towns where they originated. For example, the familiar ball-like type that we often call simply radicchio is actually radicchio di Chioggia, from the town of Chioggia near Venice, home to Chioggia beets as well. The radicchio in this dish is the long slim radicchio di Treviso named after the city in the Veneto.

I first learned to make this dish at Acquarello in San Francisco while on my internship during culinary school. I was blown away by the combination of sweet, sour, salty, and bitter all in the same bite. To this day it is one of my favorite dishes to accompany grilled or roast pork. I sometimes like to add a little bit of rendered smoked pancetta when serving this on the lunch buffet to give it the meatiness it needs when it is not accompanying an entrée.

4 heads radicchio di Treviso or radicchio di Chioggia, cored and cut into large dice

½ cup (118 ml) balsamic vinegar

½ cup (118 ml) extra virgin olive oil

6 red onions, peeled and cut into ¼-inch (.6-cm)-thick rings

Freshly ground black pepper, to taste

Preheat the oven to 350°F (177°C).

In a large bowl, toss the radicchio with ¼ cup of the balsamic vinegar and ¼ cup of the olive oil and season lightly with salt and pepper. Put the radicchio on a rimmed baking sheet lined with parchment paper (the radicchio should be fairly crowded).

In the same bowl, toss the red onions with the remaining balsamic vinegar and olive oil and season with salt and pepper. Put the onions on a rimmed baking sheet lined with parchment paper.

Bake the radicchio and the onions for about 45 minutes, stirring every 15 minutes, until they are evenly roasted and slightly caramelized.

Combine the onions and radicchio and taste and adjust the seasoning. Serve at room temperature.

PATATE E CARCIOFI AL FORNO CON OLIVE NERE

ROASTED POTATOES WITH ARTICHOKES & BLACK OLIVES

———

The combination of artichokes and olives is timeless: who knows how long Europeans have been eating these two side by side. This recipe is also a nice twist on traditional roasted potatoes. I love the distinct textures of this hearty side dish with soft roasted olives, crunchy roasted artichokes, and creamy roasted potatoes, wonderfully complemented by garlic and thyme.

4 globe artichokes, cleaned (p. 225), and lemon water reserved

6 medium potatoes (about 2.2 lbs [998 g]), peeled and cut into 1-inch (2.5-cm) wedges (keep in cold water until needed)

½ cup (118 ml) extra virgin olive oil, plus more if needed

8 thyme sprigs

4 garlic cloves, skin on, smashed

½ cup oil-cured black olives or Gaeta olives

Freshly ground black pepper, to taste

Preheat the oven to 400°F (204°C).

Bring a large pot of cold water to a boil.

Cut the artichokes into wedges similar in size to the potatoes and return them to the lemon water.

When the water comes to a rolling boil, salt it, and add the potatoes. Blanch for about 5 minutes (the potatoes should still be very firm). Remove them using a slotted spoon and transfer them to a medium bowl. Reserve the boiling water. Toss the potatoes with 6 tablespoons of the olive oil and season liberally with salt. Put the potatoes in a large rectangular baking dish; keep the bowl at hand.

Add 1½ cups of the reserved lemon water to the water used to boil the potatoes. Add the artichokes and blanch for 3 or 4 minutes, until they are slightly tender. Drain them and transfer the artichokes to the bowl used to toss the potatoes. Toss them with 2 tablespoons of the olive oil and season with salt. Scatter the artichokes, thyme, and garlic among the potatoes, creating an even layer. Make sure the potatoes aren't too crowded or they will not brown. Add more olive oil if the baking dish looks dry.

Bake for about 1 hour and 20 minutes. After the first 20 minutes, stir the potatoes and scatter in the olives. Keep stirring every 20 minutes, until the potatoes and artichokes are golden brown and crispy on the outside. Serve hot or warm with freshly ground black pepper, if you like.

CAVOLFIORE AL FORNO CON MOLLICA DI PANE E ROSMARINO FRITTO

ROASTED CAULIFLOWER WITH BREADCRUMBS & FRIED HERBS

After tasting this recipe, you'll never look at cauliflower the same way again. By roasting it, the cauliflower becomes amazingly sweet. I like to let it get a little brown and almost crunchy around the edges to play with the different textures and flavors of the vegetable: brown and roasted on the outside and meltingly tender on the inside. The addition of breadcrumbs and fried herbs adds great texture and fragrance to the dish.

1½ cups homemade breadcrumbs (p. 205)

1 large cauliflower (about 2 lbs [907 g]), sliced lengthwise ½-inch (1.3-cm)-thick

⅓ cup (79 ml) extra virgin olive oil

Freshly ground black pepper, to taste

4 cups (946 ml) vegetable oil

6 large rosemary sprigs, needles removed (about 1 cup needles)

Preheat the oven to 350°F (177°C).

In a large bowl, toss the cauliflower with the olive oil and season with salt and pepper. Scatter the cauliflower evenly on a baking sheet and roast for about 45 minutes, stirring every 15 minutes, or until it is soft, browned and slightly caramelized.

Put the vegetable oil in a small high-sided pot over medium heat. Make sure the oil does not come more than halfway up the sides of the pot. When the oil reaches 350°F (177°C), carefully lower the rosemary needles into the oil and fry them for about 45 seconds, or until the sizzling has reduced (this will happen very quickly) and the needles are crunchy. Quickly remove the needles using a slotted spoon and drain the rosemary on paper towels.

Combine the breadcrumbs and fried rosemary, mixing well and crumbling the two together with your hands. Top the cauliflower with the breadcrumbs and the fried rosemary and serve immediately.

RAPE ROSSE CON ARANCE E NOCI
ROASTED BEETS WITH ORANGES & TOASTED WALNUTS

Year after year, this is an Academy favorite. I have come to realize that beets are one of those things that people either love or hate because cooked beets often have a very peculiar earthy flavor. Nevertheless, even people who don't like beets usually fall in love with the beets at the American Academy, because of the special way we cook them. I find the pairing of beets and oranges amazing, especially when the oranges are cold from the refrigerator: the cold helps balance the natural sweet and sour flavors of the fruit to perfectly complement the sweet and sour taste of the beets. Walnuts bring warmth to the dish and add fantastic texture.

6 medium beets, roasted, cut into ¼-inch (.6-cm) dice and marinated (p. 211)

1 small bunch fennel fronds

⅓ cup (79 ml) extra virgin olive oil, plus more if necessary

3 oranges, peeled and sliced (p. 231)

1 cup walnuts, toasted and roughly chopped (p. 233)

Combine the fennel fronds and the olive oil in a small high-sided bowl and puree with a hand blender to make fennel oil. Add more olive oil if the mixture looks too thick. Season with salt and let sit for 15 minutes.

Arrange the orange slices on a platter and carefully place the diced beets (they will stain the orange if they are moved) on top of the oranges. Drizzle with the fennel oil and top with the chopped walnuts. Serve immediately.

FINOCCHIO AL FORNO
CON LIMONE E SALVIA
ROASTED FENNEL & ONIONS WITH LEMON & SAGE

——————

This is a great room-temperature side dish. The sweetness of roasted fennel is wonderfully complemented by the earthy sage, the sweet and sour perfume of the lemon peel, and the pickled roasted onions. We also like to mix this dish into boiled farro and serve it as a lunch salad on the buffet. We use such a large quantity of fennel for salads at the RSFP that we often end up with tons of fennel outer layers, which are ideal for stewing or slow roasting. We mainly prepare this dish with these tough outer layers of the fennel. Fennel outers will keep in the refrigerator for a few days if they are covered with plastic, so I recommend using fennel a few nights in a week and then making this dish when you have a nice reserve of outers. By using the tender inner fennel for salad and the tough outer leaves for roasting or broasting, you get two dishes out of one vegetable, and nothing goes to waste. How great is that?

3 fennel bulbs, trimmed and cut into ¾-inch (1.9-cm) wedges

16 sage leaves

1 lemon, zested into strips with a vegetable peeler

½ cup (118 ml) extra virgin olive oil

Freshly ground black pepper, to taste

2 medium red onions, peeled and cut into ¼-inch (.6-cm)-thick slices

2 tablespoons balsamic vinegar

Preheat the oven to 325°F (163°C).

Toss the fennel wedges with the sage leaves, lemon peel, and ¼ cup olive oil; season with salt and pepper. Spread the fennel on a rimmed baking sheet lined with parchment paper.

Toss the onions with the balsamic vinegar and ¼ cup olive oil; season with salt and pepper. Spread the onion slices on another rimmed baking sheet lined with parchment paper.

Bake the fennel and the onions for about 55 minutes, stirring every 15 minutes, until the fennel and onions are roasted and slightly caramelized.

Combine the vegetables while they are still warm, taste and adjust the seasoning, and serve hot or at room temperature.

PRIMAVERA
SPRING

By March, everyone at the Academy has grown tired of winter produce and of the whole "eating seasonally" thing. The entire community craves something new. The first vegetable that hints at the arrival of spring is green garlic. It appears in late winter and is the earliest sign of a different season right around the corner. By the time the first beautiful green asparagus, peas, and fava beans of spring arrive, people are almost weeping with joy for these new flavors. As dramatic as that may sound, they bring the promise of warmer weather, time spent outdoors, and sunshine.

Spring is a delicate and temperamental season. In Rome, it is definitely the shortest vegetable season of the year. Cooks scramble to make the most of its wonderful bounty before it gives way to summer in the blink of an eye. The microseasonality here is wildly apparent: you can actually notice a change from week to week, and in some cases even from day to day. If it's hot for four or five days in a row, lettuces bolt (they suddenly grow rapidly and start to produce seeds and flowers instead of leaves), asparagus flower, peas and favas start to get starchy. This of course affects how the vegetable needs to be cooked, so take special care to understand where it is in the season, and prepare it to maximize its natural flavor.

Spring vegetables can be labor-intensive. The interns at the RSFP spend late afternoons shelling peas, peeling fava beans, or topping and tailing green beans in the *cortile* of the Academy or in the Bass Garden. Although it is time-consuming, it is such a soothing activity that Fellows often use it to take a break from their studies and join the interns to help shell for an hour or two. That time of day is always precious as people from different walks of life come together and get to know one another or sit companionably in silence over a crate of peas.

FAGIOLINI CON AGLIO NUOVO
SAUTÉED GREEN BEANS WITH NEW GARLIC

Garlic is usually dried or cured after it is harvested to preserve it for the long winter ahead—this is the garlic we are accustomed to using year round—yet there are actually many stages of the garlic's life. New garlic is the garlic plant after it has formed a firm bulb with tiny cloves, when it still has a long green stem. As the garlic dries through the winter months, it slowly loses moisture, concentrating the essential oils in the clove, giving it a spicier and bolder taste in the mouth. However, before it dries, it is less pungent and much sweeter. New garlic is so fresh it can be peeled simply by using your fingers.

¼ cup (59 ml) extra virgin olive oil

6 new garlic cloves, peeled and chopped

2 lbs (907 g) thin green beans, topped and tailed

Bring a large pot of cold water to a boil.

Put the olive oil and the new garlic in a 14-inch (36-cm) sauté pan over medium-low heat. Cook, stirring occasionally, until it is translucent, then turn off the heat.

When the water comes to a rolling boil, salt it, and add the green beans. Cook, stirring occasionally, for about 5 minutes, or until they are tender. Drain the green beans and immediately add them to the garlic, tossing well until they are coated with the garlic and olive oil. The garlic pieces should stick to the green beans. Taste and adjust the seasoning and serve warm.

VIGNAROLA
ROMAN-STYLE SPRING VEGETABLE STEW

─────

In Rome, vignarola is the quintessential spring dish. It is quite significant to me because it takes me back to my earliest RSFP days. On February 26, 2007, when Mona Talbott and I served the very first meal of the Rome Sustainable Food Project, spring was around the corner. One day, Gianpaolo Battaglia asked me if I knew what vignarola was and if we would serve it. I had never heard of it, and in fact this dish is largely unknown outside of Rome. It also has rather mysterious origins. One version is that it is a dish typically made by a vignarola, *a woman who tends the* vigne, *or grapevines. Another is that a vegetable vendor can be called a* vignarolo, *so the dish was traditionally made by his wife to use up leftover vegetables. This is the beauty of these names: the infinite interpretations. Vignarola is particularly delicious served with a fried or poached egg.*

1 lemon (for cleaning the artichokes)

4 globe artichokes, cleaned and cut into wedges (p. 225), reserve the lemon water

1 lb (454 g) unshelled fresh peas (about 1 cup shelled)

1 lb (454 g) unshelled fresh fava beans (about 1 cup shelled)

1 bunch spring onions, peeled and thinly sliced (about 1 cup)

1 bunch green garlic, peeled and thinly sliced (about ½ cup)

½ cup (118 ml) extra virgin olive oil

5 mint sprigs, picked and chopped (about 2 teaspoons)

Bring a large pot of cold water to a boil.

When the water comes to a rolling boil, salt it, and cook the peas for 4 minutes, or until tender. Remove them using a slotted spoon and transfer them to a rimmed baking sheet to cool. Set aside 1 cup of the boiling water for later. Add the artichokes to the water with ½ cup lemon water from cleaning the artichokes. Cook them for 3 minutes, drain the artichokes, and transfer them to a baking sheet to cool. Add the fava beans to the water and cook for 3 minutes. Remove them using a slotted spoon and immediately transfer them to a bowl of ice water. Peel the fava beans by removing and discarding the tough and slightly bitter skin and gently squeezing out the bright green beans inside. If the fava beans are very small, you can keep them whole.

Put the spring onions, green garlic, and olive oil in a medium pot over medium-low heat. Add a pinch of salt and cook, stirring

*10 large romaine leaves,
cut into thin strips*

*10 parsley sprigs, picked and
chopped (about 3 tablespoons)*

occasionally, until the spring onions are translucent. Make sure you do not burn the green garlic. Add the mint and stir well. Add the artichokes and the reserved cooking water and cook, stirring occasionally, for about 12 minutes. Add the fava beans and cook for 6 more minutes. Add the peas and cook for 4 minutes, or until all the vegetables are tender. Add the romaine, stir well, then add the parsley. Taste and adjust the seasoning and serve warm.

ASPARAGI AL FORNO
CON OLIO PROFUMATO AL BASILICO
ROASTED ASPARAGUS WITH BASIL OIL

The combination of asparagus and basil is one of my absolute favorites. I only recently discovered it because, unlike in the U.S., where basil is a summer crop, in Italy we get our first basil by April, in the middle of asparagus season. The sweetness of this herb wonderfully contrasts with the grassiness of the asparagus. The very first time I had this pairing was with Domenico Cortese when we prepared green fettuccine with sautéed asparagus and basil. This dish is also excellent made with boiled or grilled asparagus, and pairs wonderfully with roasted fowl such as chicken, duck, or quail.

When making the basil oil, make sure to use a soft, buttery, extra virgin olive oil—like a Ligurian olive oil—that won't dominate the basil flavor. I also recommend serving this dish with salsa verde or salsa rustica (see pages 213 and 127 for inspiration), to which you've added lots of basil.

2 lbs (907 g) fresh asparagus, preferably young and small

⅓ cup (79 ml) extra virgin olive oil, plus 3 tablespoons

40 basil leaves

Preheat the oven to 400°F (204°C).

Snap off the tough ends of the asparagus and, if the stems are very thick, peel them.

Put ⅓ cup olive oil and the basil leaves in a high-sided bowl and puree with a hand blender to make the basil oil. Let sit for 1 hour for the basil to infuse the oil.

In a large bowl, toss the asparagus with 3 tablespoons olive oil and season liberally with salt. Lay the asparagus out in an even row on a baking sheet lined with parchment paper. Cook for about 35 minutes, or until the asparagus have browned and caramelized, carefully stirring every 15 minutes so the asparagus roast evenly.

Let the asparagus cool for 15 minutes and drizzle the basil oil over the dish. Serve warm.

ASPARAGI CON SALSA RUSTICA
ASPARAGUS WITH SALSA RUSTICA

At home I have a habit of adding an egg to just about any dish. Whether poached, fried, or hard-boiled, an egg always seems to make it better, but few things beat eggs and asparagus: the pairing is to die for. At the RSFP, we like to serve asparagus with this salsa verde that has (surprise!) hard-boiled eggs added to it. Throughout Italy, salsa verde is prepared in many different ways, but salsa rustica—salsa verde with eggs—might be my favorite.

1 batch salsa verde (p. 213)

2 bunches fresh asparagus (about 2 lbs [907 kg]), preferably thin and young

2 large eggs, room temperature

Freshly ground black pepper, to taste

2 tablespoons extra virgin olive oil

Bring a large pot of cold water to a boil.

Snap off the tough ends of the asparagus and, if the stems are very thick, peel them.

When the water comes to a rolling boil, salt it, and add the asparagus. Cook until the asparagus is tender, but still firm, about 5 minutes. Drain it and scatter the asparagus on a baking sheet to cool.

Bring a small pot of cold water to a boil. When the water comes to a rolling boil, carefully lower the eggs into the water. Simmer for 10 minutes and immediately transfer them to a bowl of ice water. Let the eggs cool for 5 minutes, drain and crack them and put them back in a bowl of tepid water for 5 more minutes. Gently peel the eggs under the water (it's easier).

Roughly chop the eggs and add them to the salsa verde. Taste and adjust the seasoning with salt and pepper.

In a large bowl toss the asparagus with the olive oil and season with salt.

To serve, lay the asparagus flat or in the shape of a fan and spoon over the salsa rustica. Top with pepper and serve at room temperature.

ASPARAGI CON BURRO SNOCCIOLATO E PARMIGIANO

ASPARAGUS WITH BROWN BUTTER & PARMESAN

————

After a long winter of eating cabbages and broccoli, asparagus seems like a godsend. The taste of asparagus is so clean and distinct; its green grassy flavor pairs nicely with the sweet nuttiness of the butter and the sharpness of the Parmesan for a wonderfully hearty dish. A delicious variation is made with asparagus roasted in the oven at 400°F with cubes of cold butter and tossed with Parmesan until a nice brown crust has formed.

2 bunches asparagus (about 2 lbs [907 kg])

8 tablespoons (113 g) butter

Freshly ground black pepper, to taste

3 oz (85 g) Parmigiano-Reggiano (about 1 cup grated)

¼ teaspoon freshly grated nutmeg, or to taste

Bring a large pot of cold water to a boil.

Snap off the tough ends of the asparagus and, if the stems are very thick, peel them.

When the water comes to a rolling boil, salt it, and add the asparagus. Cook until the asparagus is still slightly firm, about 4 minutes. Drain it and scatter the asparagus on a baking sheet to cool.

Make the brown butter: in a 14-inch (36-cm) sauté pan melt the butter over medium heat until white foam (the impurities) appears on the top. Skim the foam and discard it. Keep cooking the butter until the solids start to turn golden brown. It will have a pleasant nutty aroma. Pay close attention since the butter can go from golden brown to burnt very quickly. (If you burn the brown butter it can't be salvaged; discard it and start over.) Turn off the heat and make sure all of the white foam has carefully been removed from the surface. Immediately add the tender asparagus and gently toss it, taking care not to break any. Taste and adjust the seasoning with salt and pepper. Generously top with Parmigiano and a little grating of nutmeg and serve immediately.

RICOTTA DI PECORA
CON SALSA DI FAVE FRESCHE
SHEEP'S MILK RICOTTA
WITH FAVA BEANS, SPRING ONIONS & MINT

This is the ultimate early spring dish, made with small young fava beans that are sweet and tender. They are magnificent paired with good sweet sheep's milk ricotta and brightened by lemon and mint. Sheep's milk ricotta is very special in the spring, when, to escape the approaching summer heat, shepherds in Italy take their sheep up into the mountain valleys for the "crossing of the land" (transumanza), the biannual migration of flocks or herds from the plains to the mountains and vice versa. After eating hay during the winter, they eat fresh wild herbs, grasses, and flowers in the highlands. This change in diet makes for a more nutritious and uniquely flavored ricotta. Let the ingredients dictate the dish; don't make this unless little sweet favas are available. If you only can find the bigger starchier favas, I recommend making the fava toasts on page 134.

2 small spring onions, peeled and minced

1 lemon

1 lb (454 g) unshelled fresh fava beans (about 1 cup shelled)

15 mint sprigs, leaves picked and chopped (about 2 tablespoons)

10 parsley sprigs, leaves picked and chopped (about 3 tablespoons)

¼ cup (59 ml) extra virgin olive oil

1 lb (454 g) sheep's milk ricotta, preferably sold in its basket

Bring a medium pot of cold water to a boil.

Cover the spring onions with the juice of 1 lemon, sprinkle with salt, and macerate for 30 minutes.

When the water comes to a rolling boil, add the fava beans, and cook for 45 seconds. Drain them and transfer the fava beans to a bowl of ice water. Peel them by removing and discarding the tough and slightly bitter skin and gently squeezing out the green beans inside. If the fava beans are very small, keep them whole.

Mix the fava beans with the herbs and olive oil, and add the macerated onions (reserve the lemon juice). Taste and adjust the seasoning, adding salt or some of the remaining lemon juice as necessary.

Carefully slice the ricotta. Lay the slices on a serving plate or spoon it in dollops, and top with the fava salsa. Serve immediately.

CARCIOFINI SOTT'OLIO

BABY ARTICHOKES PRESERVED IN OIL

———

Once the largest artichoke has been harvested from the plant, it starts to produce successively smaller artichokes that are tender to their core. At the beginning of spring, Italians like to preserve these baby artichokes sott'olio, or under oil, to be enjoyed as part of a cold antipasto misto. They will keep for up to 30 days in the refrigerator. For more information on preserving, see page 191.

3 lbs (1.4 kg) baby artichokes, cleaned (p. 225)

2 lemons (one for cleaning the artichokes)

½ cup (118 ml) white wine vinegar

2 teaspoons dry oregano

20 parsley sprigs, picked and chopped (about 6 tablespoons)

1 cup (237ml) extra virgin olive oil, plus more if needed

Bring a large pot of cold water to a boil.

When the water comes to a rolling boil, add the vinegar and the baby artichokes and cook for about 15 minutes, or until they are quite tender.

Drain the artichokes and transfer them to a large baking sheet to cool.

When the artichokes are cool enough to handle, gently squeeze out any excess water, being careful not to break them.

Toss the artichokes with the oregano, parsley, juice of ½ lemon, and ½ cup olive oil in a large bowl. Taste and adjust the seasoning with salt.

Pack the artichokes tightly in a 2-quart (2-l) jar. Cover with the remaining olive oil, adding more as necessary to fill the jar. Refrigerate for at least 3 days before using.

BRUSCHETTE DI FAVE
CON CICORIA E RICOTTA SALATA
FAVA BEAN TOASTS
WITH DANDELION GREENS & RICOTTA SALATA
———

As spring progresses and the weather warms up, fava beans get bigger, and they also get starchier. The starch makes them excellent for long cooking and stewing. You can make a delicious fresh fava bean soup with pancetta as well as a fantastic puree for crostini and bruschette. I prefer a bruschetta over a crostino, because a bruschetta is a thicker piece of bread that is crunchy on the outside but remains soft and chewy on the inside (a crostino is just plain crunchy throughout). This puree is also phenomenal tossed with pasta and topped with ricotta salata. Shelling and peeling fava beans is time-consuming, but I find the whole process relaxing, and the results are well worth the time.

1 lb (454 g) dandelion greens, trimmed

3 to 4 lbs (1.4 to 1.8 kg) unshelled fresh fava beans (about 3 cups shelled)

¾ cup (177 ml) extra virgin olive oil, plus more for brushing the bruschette

1 bunch green garlic, peeled and thinly sliced (about 1 cup)

1 large rosemary sprig, needles picked and chopped (about 2 tablespoons)

1 teaspoon hot pepper flakes

6 slices day-old rustic country bread, cut ½-inch (1.3-cm)-thick

3 oz (85 g) ricotta salata, grated on a box grater using the large holes (about 1 cup)

Bring a medium pot of cold water to a boil.

When the water comes to a rolling boil, add the dandelion greens and blanch for 4 minutes or until tender. Remove them using a slotted spoon (reserve the water) and scatter the dandelion greens on a baking sheet to cool.

Add the fava beans to the same water and cook for 45 seconds. Drain the fava beans and immediately transfer them to a bowl of ice water. Peel the fava beans by removing and discarding the tough and slightly bitter skin and gently squeezing out the bright green beans inside.

Put ½ cup olive oil, half of the green garlic, and a pinch of salt in a 14-inch (36-cm) high-sided sauté pan over medium-low heat. Cook, stirring occasionally, until the green garlic is translucent.

Add the rosemary and continue cooking for 1 minute; add the fava beans and a pinch of salt, and continue cooking over medium heat until the fava beans are soft, tender, and breaking down. If you are using late-season fava beans that are slightly starchy, add 1 cup water to help them break down, adding more water if necessary, until they form a dense thick puree (some chunkiness is ok); then turn off the heat. If the fava beans haven't broken down yet but are tender, puree them in the pan using a hand blender.

Preheat the oven to 400°F (204°C).

When the dandelion greens are cool enough to handle, squeeze out any excess water and roughly chop them. Put ¼ cup olive oil in a 14-inch (36-cm) sauté pan over medium heat. When the oil is hot, add the greens and sauté for 3 minutes. Make a well in the middle of the greens and add the rest of the green garlic and let it cook until translucent. Add a pinch of hot pepper flakes and stir all the ingredients together. Taste and adjust the seasoning.

Put the slices of bread on a baking sheet and brush them with olive oil on both sides. Toast them in the oven for about 10 minutes, flipping the toasts after 6 minutes, until the outside is crunchy on both sides but the inside is still soft and chewy.

Spread a thick layer of the fava bean puree on the bread and top with the spicy sautéed greens and freshly grated ricotta salata. Serve warm or at room temperature.

PISELLI CON PROSCIUTTO
PEAS WITH PROSCIUTTO DI PARMA, CREAM & MINT

———

Peas and prosciutto is a very Roman dish, traditionally made with prosciutto di Parma and tomato sauce. That version, with tomato sauce, better lends itself to larger, starchier, late-season peas. When the very first peas of the year arrive, they are so tiny and sweet that I prefer to prepare them this way—with cream, spring onions, and herbs—to showcase their delicate sweetness. The key is to add the cream at the end and not to let it reduce very much. I like to use prosciutto di Parma here as well, but feel free to use pancetta or prosciutto cotto (Italian cooked ham).

3 tablespoons extra virgin olive oil

1 bunch spring onions, peeled and thinly sliced (about 1 cup)

2 oz prosciutto di Parma, cut into ¼-inch (.6-cm) dice

⅓ cup (79 ml) white wine, like a Chardonnay or a Verdicchio

1 cup (237 ml) heavy cream

10 parsley sprigs, picked and chopped (about 3 tablespoons)

5 thyme sprigs, picked and chopped (about 1 teaspoon)

5 mint sprigs, picked and chopped (about 2 teaspoons)

3 lbs (1.4 kg) unshelled fresh English or baby peas (about 3 cups shelled peas)

Freshly ground black pepper, to taste

Bring a medium pot of cold water to a boil.

Put the olive oil, spring onions, prosciutto, and a pinch of salt in a 12-inch (30-cm) sauté pan over medium-low heat and cook, stirring frequently, until the onions are translucent.

Add the white wine and raise the heat to medium. Reduce the wine until it has almost all evaporated.

Add the cream and chopped herbs and bring to a boil, then immediately remove from the heat without reducing the cream.

When the water comes to a rolling boil, salt it, and cook the peas for 4 to 6 minutes or until tender. Drain them and quickly transfer the peas to the sauté pan with the cream.

Place the pan over medium heat and bring it once again to a boil, then turn the heat off right away, making sure not to reduce the cream. Taste and adjust the seasoning with salt and pepper and serve immediately.

INSALATA DI PATATE

POTATO SALAD WITH CELERY, CAPERS & BLACK OLIVES

At the RSFP we make a Mediterranean-influenced potato salad using capers and olives, dressed with a mustard vinaigrette. We have the luxury of using Giovanni Bernabei's potatoes, which maintain their texture like no other. One of the tricky things with potato salad is that you have to constantly keep tasting it; one moment it seems like the salt and acidity are fine, then an hour or two later, it tastes bland. I recommend making this salad well in advance so that the flavors have time to marry and develop, and you only have to re-season it once before serving.

2 celery stalks, sliced diagonally ⅛-inch (.3-cm)-thick

2 lbs (907 g) Yukon Gold potatoes (about 6 medium potatoes)

3 tablespoons Dijon mustard

4 tablespoons white wine vinegar

Freshly ground black pepper, to taste

½ cup (118 ml) extra virgin olive oil

15 parsley sprigs, picked and chopped (about 4 tablespoons)

¼ cup salt-packed capers, rinsed and chopped (p. 229)

½ cup Gaeta olives, oven-roasted or oil-cured black olives

Bring a large pot of cold water to a boil.

When the water comes to a rolling boil, salt it, and add the celery. Blanch until it is still slightly crunchy, about 2 minutes. Remove the celery using a slotted spoon (reserve the water) and scatter it on a baking sheet to cool.

Add the potatoes to the boiling water and cook until tender, about 20 to 25 minutes. Drain them and scatter on a rimmed baking sheet to cool.

In a small bowl, combine the mustard and vinegar and season with salt and pepper. Whisk in the olive oil energetically, until the dressing has emulsified.

When the potatoes are cool enough to handle but still warm, peel them using a paring knife. Carefully cut the potatoes into ¼-inch (.6-cm)-thick slices.

In a large bowl, season the warm potatoes with salt and pepper. Whisk the mustard vinaigrette and gently toss the potatoes with it. Add the parsley, capers, celery, and olives, and mix well. Let it sit for 1 hour. Taste, adjust the seasoning, and serve at room temperature.

PATATE NOVELLE AL FORNO
BROASTED NEW POTATOES

In late May, the trustees of the American Academy arrive in Rome for end-of-the-year meetings. Every year at that time we hold a picnic dinner in the Bass Garden on Open Studios night, when the Fellows invite the trustees and the public to view their work. It's also when Giovanni Bernabei brings us his patate novelle, delightfully small potatoes the size of marbles. New potatoes are only available for about a month here in Rome, so they are a rare delicacy. The skin is so delicate and tender that even Italians, who don't like to eat potatoes with the skin, make an exception. The beauty of this recipe lies in its simplicity. We broast the new potatoes (braise and roast them) with a few whole garlic cloves added to the roasting pan to give the fragrance of garlic, but these are not actually garlicky potatoes. You will have to vary the cooking time depending on the size and type of the potato you are using.

2 lbs (907 g) new-harvest or fingerling potatoes

½ cup (118 ml) extra virgin olive oil

6 new garlic cloves, smashed with the skin on

1 large rosemary sprig, needles removed

Freshly ground black pepper, to taste

Preheat the oven to 390°F (199°C).

Wash the potatoes in lukewarm water and gently scrub them clean, taking care not to strip off the tender skin. In a medium bowl combine the olive oil, potatoes, garlic, and rosemary needles and season generously with salt and pepper. Put the potatoes in a large rectangular baking dish and add ½ cup water. Cover with aluminum foil and roast for about 40 minutes, or until easily pierced with a knife.

Uncover the potatoes and continue to roast for 20 minutes, or until crispy and golden. Serve warm.

INSALATA DI RAPE ROSSE E CETRIOLI CON SALSA VERDE ALLE MANDORLE

BEET & CUCUMBER SALAD
WITH TOASTED ALMOND SALSA VERDE

At the RSFP we prefer to grow our own beets in the Bass Garden instead of relying on our local farmers, because it can be difficult in Rome to find the age and the size of beets that we require. In spring, when the last beets are ready for harvest and the first cucumbers are coming into season, we like to serve them together with this delicious toasted almond salsa verde. This is often the Fellows' favorite salsa verde because of the amazing salty, crunchy, nutty flavor that our legendary homemade salted almonds provide in every bite. You'll be blown away by how easy these almonds are to make. This dish can be prepared largely in advance and quickly assembled if you have roasted beets and salted toasted almonds on hand.

1 batch salsa verde (p. 211)

1 bunch medium beets (about 8) roasted, cut into ⅛-inch (.3-cm)-thick slices and marinated (p. 213)

½ cup homemade toasted salted almonds, roughly chopped (to make your own see p. 207)

3 English or Japanese cucumbers, peeled, seeded, and cut into ¼-inch (.6-cm) dice

1 lemon

Freshly ground black pepper, to taste

Add the chopped almonds to the salsa verde. Taste and adjust the seasoning.

Toss the cucumbers with the juice of half a lemon and season with salt. Let marinate for 10 minutes, then add more lemon juice if necessary.

Scatter the drained marinated beets onto a serving dish. Add the diced cucumber and spoon the almond salsa verde over the vegetables. Top with pepper and serve immediately.

CONDIRE
DRESSING

Dressing lettuce can be a tricky business. At the RSFP we believe that dressing salad is an art. I know you are thinking, "please, it's just dressing lettuce!" Which of course it is, but the key to greatness lies in simplicity, and simplicity has always been a very complex thing. Here are the four most important things to consider.

First: the lettuce itself. You must think about what type it is, where it's from, and of course its maturity. No two types of lettuce should be dressed the same way: a delicate baby oak leaf lettuce needs to be dressed differently from a fully mature head of romaine or a bitter chicory like radicchio.

You will need a 2:1 ratio of oil to vinegar for little baby salads that require high acidity. If the lettuces are bigger or if you're using bitter greens, this ratio may have too much acidity and will cause the salad to seem lean; you will taste the acidity, but the salad won't feel dressed. For such lettuces you probably need closer to a 3:1 ratio of oil to vinegar, because a heartier lettuce needs more dressing.

Second: the choice of acid you want to use (usually vinegar, but lemon juice can also be fantastic). I like to use sweet vinegars such as sherry vinegar or balsamic vinegar for bitter lettuces like escarole and radicchio; red and white wine vinegars will have the highest acidity and are great for tender leaf or heads of lettuce. Avoid buying artificially flavored vinegars (such as raspberry- or mango-flavored vinegar, etc.) and stick to simple and genuine high-quality products.

Third: the type of fat. We almost always use olive oil, because in Italy no other type of oil is used for dressing salad, but others oils like grapeseed oil and hazelnut oil can be delicate and sublime. Rendered pancetta or cream can also be delicious "fats" for dressing. When using olive oil make sure it is extra virgin olive oil with a harvest date on the bottle. Extra virgin olive oil comes from the first cold pressing of the olives, which means that no heat or chemicals were used to extract the oil. This allows the nutrients and subtle aromas and flavors to remain intact. To be extra virgin, olive oil has to have less than 1% oleic acidity. This way a high concentration of solids remains in the oil, preserving the nutrients and flavors. Anything with more than 1% is simply called "olive oil" and is usually extra virgin olive oil mixed with refined, probably chemically treated oils of inferior quality. When kept under good conditions, extra virgin olive oil only lasts for about a year, so never use olive oil that is more than one year old because it is probably going rancid.

Fourth: tossing. In my opinion, it is fundamental to use your hands to toss lettuce. While many use tongs, this is an inefficient and awkward way to dress lettuce, since you can never evenly dress all the leaves and they tend to fall out of the bowl as you attempt to mix. I religiously toss lettuce with my hands.

To make the dressing, stir or whisk the vinegar with the salt. Add a smashed garlic clove or minced red or spring onions if you like and allow to macerate for 1 hour. Add the oil and whisk or stir energetically with a fork until the dressing emulsifies. The droplets of vinegar will seem suspended in the oil, and it will be noticeably creamy.

Season the lettuces with salt and freshly ground pepper and toss the salad gently with your hands. Drizzle most of the emulsified dressing onto the lettuces. Toss well with your hands starting from the bottom of the bowl and moving upwards in a circular motion so that all the leaves are evenly dressed. A perfectly dressed salad feels dressed yet balanced, not gloppy or swimming in dressing. Taste and adjust the seasoning adding more salt, pepper, or dressing as necessary. Serve immediately.

INSALATA DEL GIARDINO
GARDEN LETTUCE SALAD

Is there really anything better than lettuces freshly picked from the garden and dressed to perfection? We like to make this simple salad with the tender lettuce that we grow in the Bass Garden. A perfect salad needs the best lettuce you can find. I recommend always buying lettuce from a local farmers' market that was likely picked just hours, instead of days or even weeks, before, as is the case with supermarket lettuce. You will notice a difference; since plants start losing nutrients once they are removed from their root system, the farmer's lettuce will be more nutritious, have more flavor, and be less wilted than supermarket greens (see page 235). A perfect salad also needs to be properly dressed: see page 146 for how to dress different types of lettuces and prepare a balanced and mouthwatering salad every time.

2 lbs (907 g) lettuces, preferably oak leaf lettuce or some other small leaf mix

3 tablespoons good quality red wine vinegar

1 garlic clove, peeled and smashed

6 tablespoons good quality extra virgin olive oil

Freshly ground black pepper, to taste

Wash and dry the lettuces (p. 235).

In a large glass or measuring cup combine the red wine vinegar and garlic with a large pinch of salt and let sit for 1 hour. Remove the garlic clove and discard it. Begin adding the olive oil to the vinegar, whisking constantly, until the dressing starts to look slightly creamy and has emulsified.

Put the lettuces in a large bowl. Season with salt and pepper. Drizzle most of the emulsified dressing over the greens and toss gently from the bottom up (depending on your taste, you may not need all of the dressing). Taste and adjust the seasoning adding more salt, pepper, or dressing as needed and serve immediately.

INSALATA DI LATTUGA
CON LIMONE, PANNA E NOCCIOLE
BUTTER LETTUCE WITH LEMON, CREAM & HAZELNUTS

The simplicity of this salad is incredible. I learned to make this dish at Chez Panisse, but this salad is really an old favorite from Richard Olney, the influential American food writer and author of many important cookbooks such as The French Menu Cookbook *and* Simple French Food. *I will never forget the day I learned that heavy cream (or buttermilk or yogurt) could be used instead of oil as the fat in a dressing. It turned my world upside down. It made sense because rendered pancetta may be used as the fat in a dressing, but it had never occurred to me to use dairy in the same way.*

People tend to think that cream is heavy, and if cooked or reduced it definitely can be, but in this salad it is light and refreshing, because it is added cold from the refrigerator. Perfect on a hot spring day, this salad is delicious with any crispy head lettuce, so feel free to try it with romaine or little gem lettuces. Thinly sliced cucumbers are also a wonderful addition that I highly recommend.

2 medium heads butter lettuce	Wash and dry the lettuce (p. 235).
Freshly ground black pepper, to taste	Put the lettuce in a large bowl and season with salt and pepper. Squeeze the juice of one lemon over the lettuce and toss gently until combined. The lettuce should taste slightly acidic from the lemon. Taste and adjust the seasoning with more lemon juice or salt as necessary. Add the cream and toasted hazelnuts and toss gently to combine. Taste and adjust the seasoning once again and serve immediately.
2 lemons	
1 cup (237 ml) heavy cream	
½ cup toasted hazelnuts, chopped (p. 233)	

INSALATA DI CAROTE, SEDANO RAPA E RUCOLA

CARROT, CELERY ROOT & ARUGULA SALAD

Romans crave clean, distinct, and simple flavors—nothing overdressed, too spiced, or overly complicated. In the RSFP kitchen, we have taken this idea to heart and make sure that the flavors of our dishes remain distinct, so that each vegetable can be tasted separately in every bite. We love this kind of shaved vegetable salad at the American Academy. Adding the lemon juice to the carrots and celery root gives them an almost crunchy pickle texture, what we might even call a quick pickle. The lemon denatures the cells of the vegetable, making it flexible and snappy. Depending on the season, we like to make this salad in many different ways, at times using fennel or celery instead of celery root. We sometimes even serve this dish with little shreds of poached chicken and chopped celery to make a light, healthy, and delicious chicken salad (which is radically different from the classic mayonnaise-based version). After tasting chicken salad this way, you may never want the old one again. Every bite is clean, bright, and distinct.

3 large carrots, peeled and cut into very thin matchsticks or julienned using a mandoline

½ medium celery root, peeled and cut into very thin matchsticks or julienned using a mandoline

2 lemons

½ teaspoon hot pepper flakes or cayenne pepper

2 bunches arugula (about 4 oz [113 g]), trimmed

Freshly ground black pepper, to taste

⅓ cup (79 ml) extra virgin olive oil

Dress the carrots and celery root separately using the juice of ½ lemon and ¼ teaspoon hot pepper flakes for each one. Sprinkle with salt and gently massage the lemon juice into the vegetables. Let sit for 30 minutes, then taste and adjust the seasoning.

Dress the arugula in a large bowl with the juice of half a lemon and season with salt and pepper. Add the carrots and celery root and toss again, careful not to bruise or break any of the tender arugula leaves. Add the olive oil and toss everything gently. Taste and adjust the seasoning once again and serve immediately.

INSALATA DI CICORIA
CON PECORINO E NOCCIOLE
DANDELION GREENS SALAD
WITH PECORINO & TOASTED HAZELNUTS

We grow dandelion greens every year at the Academy not only because they are native to the region and easy to grow with little or no maintenance, but also because the plant rebounds quickly after harvesting. This allows us to get many harvests from a single crop over the course of a season. The dandelion greens are perfect for this salad when they're small but stout. This salad is best made with the red veined varietal. It is also great when made with any bitter greens such as arugula or frisée; it's delicious dressed with the pancetta vinaigrette on page 49.

⅓ *cup (79 ml) red wine vinegar*

2 garlic cloves, peeled and smashed

1 cup (237 ml) extra virgin olive oil

Freshly ground black pepper, to taste

1 lb (454 g) baby dandelion greens, or other bitter greens such as arugula

1 cup toasted hazelnuts, roughly chopped (p. 233)

3 oz (85 g) chunk of pecorino toscano, shaved with a peeler

Prepare the dressing: in a large glass or measuring cup combine the red wine vinegar and garlic along with a large pinch of salt. Let sit for 30 minutes.

Add the olive oil and some pepper to the vinegar. Stir or whisk the dressing energetically until an emulsion has formed.

Put the dandelion greens in a large bowl and season lightly with salt and pepper. Drizzle the dressing on the greens and toss gently (you may not need all of the dressing). Taste and adjust the seasoning.

Add the toasted hazelnuts and toss again. Top with shaved pecorino toscano and serve immediately.

ESTATE

ESTATE
SUMMER

Toward the end of May, as evenings become warm, we move all the tables outside into the *cortile* of the Academy for al fresco dining during the summer months. The community loves eating outside while the sun sets, sharing one big, long convivial table. I find that summer at the Academy is always a bittersweet season, filled with nostalgia as year-long collaborations end and Fellows return home, with memories of lifelong friendships that came to be during those warm evening dinners in the courtyard.

Summer is about the sun, and the bounty that comes from the sunshine and heat. In Italy, the hot sun gives us sweet peppers, cucumbers, tomatoes, eggplant, zucchini....By the end of summer, there is such a wealth of produce that we preserve it for the cold winter months: we jar tomatoes, put zucchini and eggplant sott'olio, fire-roast our bell peppers, and dry the hot peppers.

Rome gets so hot in the summer that we crave food that is cool, light, and refreshing. It gets so hot, in fact, that at the RSFP we cook in the oven or over burners only during the early morning, when the kitchen is still relatively cool. We keep our summer dishes simple; not much has to be done to showcase the delicious natural flavors of the fruits or vegetables because the produce is just phenomenal. Think of the best summer dishes that require little to no cooking, like prosciutto e melone, caprese or panzanella; they are incredibly simple yet outstanding.

INSALATA DI POMODORI

TOMATO SALAD

———

There is no greater satisfaction than going out into the Bass Garden early in the morning to harvest our organically grown tomatoes to serve on the lunch buffet. For this salad, use sweet, juicy tomatoes only during those few weeks each year in which they are perfectly ripe. I like to use a few different types of tomatoes, to capture the variations in taste, texture, and color, and to showcase the unique qualities of each varietal. While the quality of ingredients is always important, in this case it is of the utmost importance, since in this simple recipe there's no dressing or other ingredients to enhance the taste of the tomatoes.

1 lb (454 g) beefsteak or heirloom tomatoes, cored and cut into ⅛-inch (.3-cm)-thick slices

Freshly ground black pepper, to taste

½ lb (227 g) medium Early Girl tomatoes, cored and cut into wedges

20 small Italian basil leaves

¼ cup (59 ml) extra virgin olive oil

½ lb (227 g) mixed cherry tomatoes, cut in half

Arrange the tomato slices on a large platter and season them with salt and pepper.

In a medium bowl, toss the tomato wedges with salt, 10 basil leaves, and 2 tablespoons olive oil. Let sit for 5 minutes.

In another bowl, toss the cherry tomatoes with salt, the remaining basil, and the remaining olive oil. Let sit for 5 minutes.

Spoon the tomato wedges and then the cherry tomatoes (with some of the tomato juices) over the sliced tomatoes, grind some pepper on top, and serve immediately.

INSALATA CAPRESE
TOMATO & MOZZARELLA SALAD

I am always amazed at how much I have learned while living in Italy. I was accustomed, as most of us are, to using perfectly ripe, sweet tomatoes for a caprese. I was proven wrong one day by a seventeenth-generation Roman who is also half Neapolitan and therefore can speak with some authority about this salad, which is originally from the island of Capri, off of the Amalfi Coast near Naples.

In southern Italy, insalata caprese is almost always served with semi-green tomatoes, and this is intentional. Unripe tomatoes—and some specific varietals, such as Aunt Ruby's German green or green Zebras—have higher acidity than juicy red slicing tomatoes. Buffalo milk mozzarella is quite rich, and if served with a ripe sweet tomato and with sweet basil, the dish can just fall flat. A more acidic varietal or the acidity of a slightly under-ripe tomato brings out the distinct flavors of each ingredient in the dish. It cuts through the richness of the mozzarella and improves the overall "edibility" of the dish, as we like to say in the kitchen. Now, combine great slightly acidic tomatoes, sweet basil, and delicious mozzarella with a really good extra virgin olive oil...you've turned a good caprese into an unbelievable caprese. If you're still skeptical, try a side-by-side comparison with different tomatoes and you'll see exactly what I mean. Leave the mozzarella out for an hour or so before serving it—the protein in the mozzarella relaxes, making it more tender.

2 large high-acid or slightly under-ripe tomatoes (about 1 lb [454 g]), cored and cut into ⅛-inch (.3-cm)-thick slices

2 medium balls fresh buffalo milk mozzarella, about 1 lb (454 g), cut into ⅛-inch (.3-cm)-thick slices

15 small Italian basil leaves

3 to 4 tablespoons extra virgin olive oil

Spread the tomato slices out on a cutting board or on a plate. Season with salt, then alternate slices of tomatoes and mozzarella on a platter.

Tear the basil leaves and scatter them over the tomatoes and mozzarella. Drizzle the olive oil over the salad and serve immediately.

PANZANELLA

TUSCAN-STYLE BREAD SALAD

———

There are a million different versions and interpretations of panzanella. Authentic panzanella is from Tuscany and requires only a few simple ingredients: unsalted Tuscan bread, excellent Tuscan olive oil, tomatoes, red onions, basil, and a touch of good red wine vinegar. Pane sciapo or pane sciocco is the unsalted bread typical of certain areas of Tuscany, Umbria, and the Marche. There are many stories about why bread was made without salt during the Middle Ages and the Renaissance, but what I find most surprising is that, to this day, this tradition has endured, and people from those regions still largely prefer their bread without salt. Originally panzanella was a peasant's dish in which stale pane sciapo was tossed with whatever was left over, which often included raw onions. Traditionally, the bread is soaked with the juice of tomatoes, water, and vinegar to soften it and then squeezed, crumbled, and tossed with tomatoes.

Since unsalted bread is very difficult to find in the United States and in many other countries, our version is made with croutons of salted whole-grain bread from Lariano, a region in Lazio, and is more of a bread salad than an authentic panzanella. I think you will find this version delicious. One of the most important things to consider is the type of extra virgin olive oil used. This is a Tuscan dish, so make sure to use Tuscan olive oil because of its bold, grassy characteristics.

1 batch croutons (see p. 203)

½ small red onion, peeled and thinly sliced

2 to 3 tablespoons red wine vinegar

5 ripe Early Girl tomatoes, cored and cut into wedges

15 Italian basil leaves, torn

¼ cup (59 ml) Tuscan extra virgin olive oil

Put the onions, vinegar, and a pinch of salt in a small bowl. Macerate the onions in the vinegar for 45 minutes.

Combine the tomatoes, basil, onions (reserving the liquid), and olive oil in a medium bowl.

After 10 minutes, add the croutons and toss well. Let sit for 30 minutes so that the croutons become slightly soft and start to absorb the tomato juices. Taste and adjust the seasoning, adding more vinegar from the macerated onions as necessary. Serve at room temperature.

POMODORI RIPIENI
HERB-STUFFED BAKED TOMATOES

This is an adaptation of pomodori al riso, tomatoes stuffed with rice, which I learned to make at Chez Panisse. It is one of the best summer side dishes you can possibly make because it is incredibly simple, quick to prepare, and can be served warm or at room temperature. When the stuffed tomatoes are broken open with a knife and fork, they will burst open, revealing fleshy tomato pulp, a dense herb salsa, and crunchy breadcrumbs. They are fantastic served at room temperature with a cold roast and green beans on a hot summer evening, just as we do at the Academy in the last days of July.

6 medium Early Girl tomatoes

1 garlic clove, peeled and minced

30 parsley sprigs, picked and chopped (about ¼ cup)

30 Italian basil leaves, chopped (about ¼ cup)

¾ cup homemade breadcrumbs (see p. 205)

¼ cup (59 ml) extra virgin olive oil, plus 1 tablespoon

Preheat the oven to 350°F (177°C).

Core the tomatoes by cutting a large ring around the top of each tomato. Gently squeeze any juice into a small bowl, making sure not to break the skin of the tomato. Strain the juice with a fine mesh strainer to remove the seeds and reserve the juice for later. Season the cavity of the tomatoes with salt, place them upside down on a baking sheet to remove excess juice, and let sit for 20 minutes.

In a medium bowl combine the garlic, parsley, basil, breadcrumbs, and olive oil. Stuff the tomatoes with the herb and breadcrumb mixture.

Put the strained tomato juice and 1 tablespoon of olive oil into a small casserole or gratin dish. Pack the stuffed tomatoes tightly into the baking dish. Bake for 45 minutes or until the tomatoes are very soft. Let cool for 20 minutes and serve warm or at room temperature.

INSALATA COMPOSTA
DI FAGIOLI BORLOTTI FRESCHI
CON POMODORI E MOLLICA DI PANE

FRESH BORLOTTI BEANS WITH HEIRLOOM TOMATOES,
BREADCRUMBS & AÏOLI

———

This may be my favorite summer salad. I absolutely love fresh shell beans. They have a much thinner and more delicate skin than dried beans, and their creaminess is sublime. One of the things that draws me back to this dish is the fantastic mixture of textures and flavors. The breadcrumbs contrast wonderfully with the creaminess of the beans and the silkiness of the aïoli. Aïoli is a nice change from using olive oil, which is the usual way a bean salad is dressed. Dry shell beans may be substituted for fresh ones, but they must be soaked overnight. If dried beans are used, the overall cooking time nearly triples.

1 batch aïoli (see p. 201)

2 shallots or 1 small red onion, peeled and minced

½ cup (118 ml) red wine vinegar

3 large heirloom or beefsteak tomatoes, cored and cut into ¼-inch (.6-cm)-thick slices

Freshly ground black pepper, to taste

3 cups cooked fresh Borlotti or cannellini beans (see p. 219)

3 tablespoons extra virgin olive oil

1 summer savory sprig, picked and chopped (about 1 teaspoon) or 8 Italian basil leaves, chopped

1 cup homemade breadcrumbs (see p. 205)

In a small bowl, combine the shallots or onion and red wine vinegar with a pinch of salt and let macerate for 45 minutes.

Arrange the sliced tomatoes on a platter and season them with salt and pepper. Let sit for 5 minutes to absorb the salt.

Toss the shell beans with olive oil, salt, pepper, herbs, and the macerated onions (reserving the liquid). Taste and adjust the seasoning, adding some vinegar from the onions if necessary. Scatter the beans over the sliced tomatoes.

Top with breadcrumbs, drizzle with the aïoli, and serve immediately.

INSALATA DI ZUCCHINE
CON RUGHETTA E RICOTTA SALATA
SHAVED ZUCCHINI SALAD WITH ARUGULA, MINT,
PINE NUTS & RICOTTA SALATA

———

This is a fantastically refreshing raw zucchini salad. Mona Talbott, the executive chef at the RSFP for five years, loves this salad because it contains only raw vegetables tossed with nuts, herbs, and cheese. It is extremely healthy, and is also very interesting to eat because of its great texture. Mona also loves it because it's a very beautiful salad, with long wide ribbons of zucchini that look like bows on a Christmas present. Dressing the zucchini with salt and lemon juice a few minutes before serving allows them to almost quick pickle, and the key is to serve the salad right at the point when the ribbons have just softened and become flexible. The ricotta salata's slight creaminess rounds out the different flavors in this salad, and adds just enough richness so that it doesn't taste "lean."

¼ cup pine nuts

4 medium zucchini, shaved lengthwise with a mandoline or very thinly sliced lengthwise

1 or 2 lemons

2 mint sprigs, leaves picked and chopped

20 parsley sprigs, leaves picked and roughly chopped (about 6 tablespoons)

1 bunch of arugula (about 2 oz [57 g]), trimmed

¼ cup (59 ml) extra virgin olive oil

Freshly ground black pepper, to taste

2 oz (57 g) ricotta salata, grated using the large holes of a box grater (about 1 cup)

Preheat the oven to 300°F (149°C).

Toast the pine nuts on a baking sheet for about 7 minutes, or until they are fragrant and lightly golden.

Gently toss the zucchini in a large bowl with the juice of 1 lemon and season with salt. Add the mint and parsley, toss again, and let sit for 10 minutes.

Add the arugula, olive oil, and pine nuts and gently toss the salad together.

Taste and adjust the seasoning with lemon juice, salt, and pepper. Top with the grated ricotta salata and serve immediately.

ZUCCHINE ALLA SCAPECE
FRIED ZUCCHINI WITH VINEGAR & HOT PEPPER

———

Scapece (or escabeche in Spanish) is a method of preservation typically used for fish or vegetables that the Arabs introduced to the countries of the Mediterranean during the Moorish conquests. The preparation often includes cooking the fish or vegetables first and then marinating them in vinegar. Here, the addition of hot pepper flakes and mint gives the fried zucchini a fantastic heating and cooling effect. This dish can be prepared and eaten right away, but it is best left to sit for at least a few hours. This is an excellent side dish or accompaniment to a mixed antipasto.

3 quarts (2.8 l) vegetable oil

1 garlic clove, peeled

⅓ cup (79 ml) red wine vinegar

8 medium zucchini, cut into ⅛-inch (.3-cm)-thick coins

8 mint sprigs, picked and chopped (about 4 teaspoons)

1 teaspoon hot pepper flakes

Put a medium high-sided pot of vegetable oil over medium heat. Make sure the oil does not go more than halfway up the side of the pot.

Pound the garlic in a mortar and pestle with a pinch of salt. Combine the pounded garlic and red wine vinegar in a small bowl.

When the oil reaches 350°F (177°C), gently lower about a third of the zucchini slices in the frying oil and cook for 2 or 3 minutes or until golden. Remove the zucchini using a slotted spoon and drain them on paper towels. Sprinkle with salt. Repeat this process until all the zucchini are fried.

Put the cooled zucchini in a medium bowl and toss with the garlicky vinegar, mint, and hot pepper. Taste and adjust the seasoning and let marinate at room temperature for a few hours before serving.

ZUCCHINE SALTATE CON GREMOLATA
PAN-FRIED ZUCCHINI WITH GARLIC, PARSLEY & LEMON ZEST

Gremolata *is a condiment traditionally added to rich northern Italian dishes such as osso buco, risotto alla Milanese, roasts, and other braised meats. It is most often made with a mix of lemon zest, garlic, and parsley chopped together so that the essential oils of the ingredients mix and bring a touch of brightness and freshness. At the RSFP we like to use* gremolata *with vegetables, since it brings to them a new complexity. There are many versions of* gremolata *(we also use an orange and hazelnut one with Jerusalem artichokes, p. 105), but the* gremolata *used here is more traditional. A little trick is to sizzle the* gremolata *directly in the excess oil in the pan, because, as I always like to remind the RSFP interns, fat bonds with fat. The essential oils of the* gremolata *bind with the fat in the olive oil and infuse it. This really opens up the fragrance of the* gremolata *and helps deepen the dish's flavors.*

20 parsley sprigs, picked and finely chopped (about 6 tablespoons)

2 garlic cloves, peeled and minced

Zest of 1 lemon, minced

Freshly ground black pepper, to taste

¼ cup (59 ml) extra virgin olive oil

2 lbs (907 g) zucchini, cut into 1-inch (2.5-cm) dice

Combine the parsley, garlic, and lemon zest and roughly chop them together. Add pepper if you like and set the mixture aside in a small bowl.

Put the olive oil and zucchini in a large high-sided sauté pan over medium-high heat. Sauté the zucchini for about 15 minutes, or until they are soft and golden brown. Season with salt.

Add the gremolata to the pan and toss well. Let the gremolata sizzle in the pan with the zucchini for about 30 seconds, then turn off the heat. Taste and adjust the seasoning with salt and pepper, and serve immediately.

MELANZANE AL FUNGHETTO
EGGPLANT COOKED LIKE MUSHROOMS

This is a classic technique for cooking mushrooms throughout southern Italy, and this dish literally translates to "eggplant cooked like mushrooms." It is called this because not only does the eggplant turn brown and look like a mushroom, but the final texture is also similar to that of a mushroom. This is an impressive dish, yet it is incredibly fast and easy to prepare. You can make it in advance since it benefits from sitting as the flavors meld together.

⅓ cup (79 ml) extra virgin olive oil

4 garlic cloves, peeled and smashed

2 large Italian eggplants (about 2 lbs [907 g]), peeled and cut into ½-inch (1.3-cm) dice

20 heirloom cherry tomatoes, cut in half

20 parsley sprigs, picked and chopped (about 6 tablespoons)

1 or 2 tablespoons red wine vinegar

Put the olive oil and garlic in a 16-inch (41-cm) sauté pan over medium heat and fry the garlic until it is light golden, then remove and discard it.

Add the eggplant and sauté, stirring occasionally, for about 15 minutes, or until the eggplant has softened and is slightly browned. Season with salt.

Add the cherry tomatoes and more olive oil if the pan looks dry. Sauté for 5 minutes, or until just barely soft.

Add the chopped parsley and 1 tablespoon red wine vinegar. Taste and adjust the seasoning with salt and more red wine vinegar. Serve at room temperature.

MELANZANE ALLA PARMIGIANA DI CHRIS BEHR

CHRIS BEHR'S EGGPLANT PARMESAN

The RSFP sous-chef Chris Behr showed me this mouthwatering adaptation of an eggplant parmesan that he used to make at the Brooklyn Larder in New York. It combines all the ingredients and spirit of a delicious eggplant parmesan, but is a little bit lighter since the eggplant isn't fried, as it usually is, and there isn't any mozzarella or breadcrumbs. Chris says that the key to making this so tasty is to make it in layers and to drizzle a good bit of extra virgin olive oil in between the layers, adding basil only in the very middle layer of the dish.

3 large Italian eggplants (about 3 lbs [1.4 kg]), peeled, leaving strips of skin, and cut into 1-inch (2.5-cm) dice

1 cup (237 ml) extra virgin olive oil

1 medium onion, peeled and cut into ¼-inch (.6-cm) dice

3 garlic cloves, peeled and chopped

1 teaspoon hot pepper flakes

30 Italian basil leaves

2 lbs (907 g) fresh San Marzano-style tomatoes, cut in half

3 oz (85 g) Parmigiano-Reggiano, grated (about 1 cup)

Preheat the oven to 375°F (190°C).

In a large bowl, toss the eggplant with ¼ cup (59 ml) olive oil and season liberally with salt. Spread the eggplant out on a baking sheet lined with parchment paper. Bake for 45 minutes, rotating the sheet if necessary to ensure even cooking, until the eggplant is soft, golden, and slightly caramelized.

Put ¼ cup (59 ml) olive oil and onion in a large high-sided pot over medium-low heat. Season with salt and cook, stirring occasionally, until the onions are translucent. Make a well in the middle of the onions and add the chopped garlic, hot pepper flakes, and 5 basil leaves and sizzle for 45 seconds. Immediately add the tomatoes and simmer until the tomato has turned into a sauce. Cook for 45 minutes, or until the sauce has reduced by half. Pass the tomato sauce through a food mill and discard the fibrous leftovers of the tomato skins, or puree it with a hand blender and pass it through a fine mesh strainer.

Put 1 tablespoon olive oil and ¼ cup (59 ml) tomato sauce in the bottom of a medium rectangular baking dish. Put half of the eggplant in one even layer across the bottom. Scatter the basil leaves evenly and drizzle with 2 tablespoons olive oil. Add another ¾ cup (177 ml) tomato sauce. Cover evenly with ½ cup Parmigiano, and drizzle with 2 tablespoons of olive oil. Repeat with another layer of eggplant, the rest of the tomato sauce, and olive oil.

Bake for 35 minutes, or until it is golden brown and the edges are bubbling. Remove from the oven and top with the remaining Parmigiano. Cool before serving.

MELANZANE
CON CETRIOLI, YOGURT E MENTA
ROASTED EGGPLANT WITH CUCUMBERS, YOGURT & MINT

———

This is a Greek-inspired dish and it is pure heaven. In summer, when the sweltering heat and humidity of Rome become unbearable, we roast the eggplant as early as possible in the morning before it gets too hot in the kitchen. The minty yogurt is incredibly refreshing paired with the roasted eggplant and lemony cucumbers. Mona Talbott, the former executive chef of the RSFP, pounds the mint in a mortar and pestle, which, when mixed with the yogurt, turns it a beautiful green.

2 large Italian eggplants (about 2 lbs [907 g]), peeled, leaving strips of skin, and cut into ¼-inch (.6-cm)-thick slices

⅓ cup (79 ml) extra virgin olive oil, plus 2 tablespoons

15 mint sprigs, picked

1½ cups whole plain yogurt

Freshly ground black pepper, to taste

2 medium English or Japanese cucumbers, peeled and thinly sliced

1 lemon

Preheat the oven to 375°F (190°C).

In a large bowl, toss the eggplant slices with ¼ cup of the olive oil and season liberally with salt. Spread the slices out on a baking sheet lined with parchment paper. Bake for 45 minutes, rotating the sheet if necessary to ensure even cooking, until the eggplant is soft, golden, and slightly caramelized.

Pound the mint leaves in a mortar and pestle with a pinch of salt until it has formed a smooth paste, or finely chop the leaves. Add the mint paste to the yogurt along with 2 tablespoons of the olive oil and adjust the seasoning with salt and pepper. Let sit for 30 minutes, so the mint can infuse the yogurt.

In a medium bowl, marinate the cucumbers with the juice of 1 lemon and season with salt. Let sit for 5 to 10 minutes.

When the eggplant is cool enough to handle, arrange it in overlapping slices on a platter. Scatter the cucumbers all over the roasted eggplant.

Drizzle the mint yogurt evenly over the eggplant and cucumbers and serve immediately.

CAPONATA DI VERDURE ESTIVE
SUMMER VEGETABLE CAPONATA

———

Caponata is traditionally made with summer's bounty. When made correctly it can be an absolute revelation: somehow, despite there being so many ingredients, you can taste each one distinctly. Because caponata is traditionally from Sicily, and Sicilians love to fry food, the vegetables are usually fried. At the RSFP, we prefer to roast some of the vegetables because it makes for a lighter dish. Just like potato salad or eggplant parmesan, caponata is better the next day, once the flavors have come together. I like to use white wine vinegar to plump the raisins, but I prefer to use red wine vinegar in the dish itself because I think its acidity matches up nicely with the prevalent tomato flavor.

¼ cup golden raisins

¾ cup (177 ml) dry white wine

¼ cup (59 ml) white wine vinegar

1 large Italian eggplant (about 1 lb [454 g]), peeled, leaving strips of skin, and cut into 1-inch (2.5-cm) dice

¾ cup (177 ml) extra virgin olive oil

3 celery stalks, cut diagonally into ⅛-inch (.3-cm) slices

2 medium yellow onions, peeled and cut into ¼-inch (.6-cm) dice

¼ cup Gaeta olives or brined black olives

3 tablespoons salt-packed capers, rinsed and chopped (see p. 229)

¼ cup (59 ml) red wine vinegar, plus more if necessary

In a small pot, combine the raisins, 1½ cups water, the white wine, and the white wine vinegar. Bring to a boil and turn off the heat. Allow the raisins to plump in the liquid for 25 minutes away from the heat source.

Preheat the oven to 350°F (177°C).

Bring a medium pot of cold water to a boil.

Toss the eggplant with ¼ cup (59 ml) of the olive oil and season with salt. Roast for 35 to 45 minutes, rotating the sheet if necessary to ensure even cooking or until the eggplant is soft, creamy, and slightly caramelized. Stir the eggplant after 20 minutes.

When the water comes to a rolling boil, salt it and cook the celery for 3 minutes, or until it is tender but still crunchy.

Put ¼ cup (59 ml) of the olive oil and the onion in a 12-inch (30-cm) sauté pan over medium-low heat and add a pinch of salt. Cook, stirring occasionally, until the onions are translucent. Add the olives, capers, and the

6 garlic cloves,
peeled and smashed

3 large red bell peppers,
seeded and cut into
½-inch (1.3-cm) tiles

4 zucchini, cut into
¼-inch (.6-cm) dice

30 cherry tomatoes, cut in half

30 Italian basil leaves

¼ cup pine nuts

celery and combine well. Cook for 5 minutes, then add the red wine vinegar. Set the mixture aside.

Put ¼ cup (59 ml) of the olive oil, the garlic, and the peppers in a 14-inch (36-cm) high-sided sauté pan over medium heat. Sauté, stirring occasionally, for 25 minutes, or until the peppers are tender. Add the zucchini to the peppers and sauté for 7 more minutes.

Add the cherry tomatoes and cook for 3 minutes over high heat. Add the onion mixture and taste and adjust the seasoning, adding more red wine vinegar if necessary.

Add the roasted eggplant, the basil, the pine nuts, and the raisins (without the plumping liquid). Toss all the ingredients together and simmer for about 5 minutes, stirring frequently to prevent sticking. Taste and adjust the seasoning, put aside and allow to cool. Serve at room temperature.

FRIGITELLE RIPASSATE IN PADELLA
PAN-FRIED GREEN PEPPERS

———

This super simple recipe is a great addition to a mixed antipasto plate and is delicious served with roast chicken. Frigitelle are a unique pepper varietal that we get at the RSFP. They are similar to the pimiento de Padròn that you might find in Spain or in California, yet they are longer and fleshier. The key is to fry them slowly not only to brown them but to cook the flesh through as well. Make sure not to let the oil in the pan smoke; if it does, the heat is too high and the peppers are cooking too quickly. Since salt extracts moisture, I like to season them with salt only at the very end of cooking, so that the peppers don't weep water as they cook. Using a flaky salt at the end adds a pleasant texture.

1 lb (454 g) frigitelle, pimientos de Padròn, or other small mild or sweet green peppers

3 tablespoons extra virgin olive oil

Fleur de sel or Maldon salt, to taste

Put the olive oil and peppers in a large cast-iron pan over medium-low heat. Fry the peppers slowly, for about 20 minutes, or until they are soft, tender, fully cooked, and largely browned, turning them occasionally.

Sprinkle with fleur de sel and serve warm or at room temperature.

INSALATA DI VERZA CON PEPERONI E CIPOLLE DI TROPEA

CABBAGE SALAD WITH BELL PEPPERS & RED ONIONS

Since cabbage is available almost year round, the cabbage salad at the RSFP changes according to the season. This is delicious in the summer when peppers haven't quite fully ripened and the first summer cabbages start to arrive. In the winter, we like to make it with julienned carrots and celery root. Apples, corn, radishes, jicama, kohlrabi, shallots, raisins, and cilantro are all perfect additions depending on the season. Red cabbage is a fantastic, slightly sweeter, alternative to green cabbage. You can also substitute cider vinegar for the white wine vinegar. Salting and pressing the cabbage gives it that coleslaw-like texture because the salt denatures the cell structure of the cabbage, allowing it to become flexible while remaining crunchy.

1 green cabbage (about 2⅓ lbs [1,1 kg], cored and thinly sliced

1 medium red onion, peeled and sliced paper thin with a knife or mandoline

¾ cup (177 ml) white wine vinegar

1 large red or yellow bell pepper, cut into ⅛-inch (.3-cm)-thick slices

½ cup (118 ml) extra virgin olive oil

20 parsley sprigs, picked and chopped (about 6 tablespoons)

Freshly ground black pepper, to taste

Put the sliced cabbage in a strainer. Season generously with salt and toss well. Place a heavy weight (like a plate topped with a large can of tomatoes or bottle of olive oil) on the cabbage, so that it is pressed down, weeps its juices, and becomes tender. Keep the cabbage weighed down for 1 hour, tossing it and squeezing it every 20 minutes.

In a small bowl, macerate the onions and the white wine vinegar with a large pinch of salt for 45 minutes.

In a large bowl, combine the onions (reserving the liquid) with the peppers, season with salt, and macerate for another 15 minutes.

Add the drained cabbage and toss well. Taste and adjust the seasoning with salt and some of the remaining vinegar from the onions. Add the olive oil, parsley, and pepper and toss well. Let the salad sit for 15 minutes, taste and adjust the seasoning again, and serve.

PORRI CON SALSA ROMESCO E RUCOLA
LEEKS WITH ROMESCO & ARUGULA

Romesco sauce is a traditional Spanish sauce composed of toasted nuts, dried chilies, and breadcrumbs. We like to serve this version at the RSFP because it uses almonds and hazelnuts, which are typical ingredients in Italian cooking. Traditionally, in a salsa romesco, the nuts and breadcrumbs are fried, but we prefer to toast them, which results in a lighter dish. Romesco sauce is delicious with grilled leeks, spring onions, or scallions. We make this dish most often in the late spring and early summer, when the first peppers have started to appear, and when we have tiny leeks that fit so nicely on a plate or platter.

½ batch roasted and marinated red peppers (see p. 209)

1 batch romesco (see p. 216)

4 medium leeks

1 lb (454 g) arugula, trimmed

2 tablespoons olive oil

Bring a large pot of cold water to a boil.

Cut the leeks on the bias into ½-inch (1.3-cm) slices. Carefully wash the leeks very well in plenty of lukewarm water to get rid of any sand or dirt that may be caught in the layers.

When the water comes to a rolling boil, salt it and add the leeks. Cook, stirring occasionally, until the leeks are tender and slightly translucent, about 4 minutes. It is important that the leeks are not crunchy or mushy, but just tender. Remove the leeks using a slotted spoon and spread them out on a baking sheet to cool.

In a large bowl toss the arugula with 2 tablespoons olive oil and sprinkle with salt. Add the roasted peppers.

Spread the leeks out in an even layer on a plate or platter. Stir the romesco well before using and dot the leeks generously with romesco sauce. Top with arugula and roasted peppers and serve.

SOTT'OLIO

In Italian, to put something sott'olio means to put it under oil, or to preserve it in oil. Traditionally, preserving vegetables in Italy has been a very important way to preserve produce to eat during the winter months, and this custom is still very popular today. Many Italian families have a small vegetable garden at home called an *orto* where they grow a variety of seasonal produce. By late summer, when the hot sun has ripened an abundance of fruits and vegetables, it's time to preserve them.

Every year we make homemade jams with the fruit from the Bass Garden and can our own tomatoes to use throughout the coming year. Yet preserving isn't only about long-term storage. We like to preserve vegetables for short-term consumption as well. Covering something with oil and adding a little vinegar marinates and preserves it for a short period of time. The oil keeps air out and the vinegar prevents bacterial growth. When properly refrigerated, vegetables sott'olio will keep for up to three weeks. At the RSFP we preserve many vegetables this way, such as roasted peppers, cipolline in agrodolce, zucchine, and melanzane sott'olio. Italians love to use verdure sott'olio for a quick bite with a drink during aperitivo or on an antipasto plate.

Vegetables may also be preserved for a longer period of time—usually a year but sometimes even longer—when jars are sterilized and processed in a water bath, the method we use with our RSFP Jarred Tomatoes (see page 197). In addition to the instructions provided in the following recipes, I suggest reading up on canning and long-term preserving techniques. There are many authoritative books and online sources that provide important and helpful information about this satisfying and rewarding process.

MELANZANE SOTT'OLIO
MARINATED EGGPLANT

I learned this excellent method to preserve eggplant while living in Molise. The family I lived with used to salt and press the eggplant for 3 to 5 days to make sott'olio; however, I have found that blanching the eggplant in acidulated water, as we do at the RSFP, produces the same texture with less of a time investment. Melanzane sott'olio will keep well for at least 2 weeks, covered, in the refrigerator. I recommend letting it sit in the fridge for at least 48 hours before serving so the flavors can come together.

2 cups (473 ml) white wine vinegar

3 large Italian eggplants (about 3 lbs [1.4 kg]), peeled, sliced, and cut into ⅛-inch (.3-cm) julienne

8 mint sprigs, picked and chopped (about 2 tablespoons)

10 parsley sprigs, picked and chopped (about 3 tablespoons)

10 Italian basil leaves, chopped (about 1 tablespoon)

¼ cup (59 ml) freshly squeezed lemon juice (about 2 lemons)

½ teaspoon hot pepper flakes

1½ cups (355 ml) extra virgin olive oil

Bring a large pot of cold water to a boil. When it comes to a rolling boil, lightly salt it and add the vinegar. Blanch the eggplant for 2 minutes, or until it is translucent.

Remove it using a slotted spoon and scatter the eggplant strips on a baking sheet to cool.

When the eggplant is cool enough to handle, place it in a clean kitchen towel and squeeze out any remaining liquid. The liquid will have an almost gelatinous quality.

Put the eggplant in a large bowl and add the chopped herbs, lemon juice, and hot pepper. Toss well, and let sit for 5 minutes. Add the olive oil and toss well again. Let sit covered in the refrigerator for at least a few hours before serving.

CIPOLLINE IN AGRODOLCE
CIPOLLINI ONIONS IN SWEET & SOUR SAUCE

Cipolline in agrodolce are often served in Rome as part of a buffet antipasto. They are a delicious sweet and sour dish that cuts through other rich flavors of a mixed antipasto, and make an excellent accompaniment to a good roast served at room temperature in the summer. Another plus: during the stifling Roman summer, these refreshing, almost pickled onions keep well for several days. At the RSFP we typically make a large batch so that we don't have to heat up the kitchen repeatedly.

Make sure the onions are cooked only until they are barely tender in the middle, and easily pierced with a small knife. As the onions sit overnight, they will firm up as the vinegar slightly pickles them (but in this recipe, with less acid and more sugar than a typical pickle). The cooked vinegar should be thick and syrupy and sweet and sour. If you like a crunchier onion, cook them a little less; in Rome they are served crisp yet nearly tender to the core. If you are making a big batch, make sure you cool the cipolline completely before refrigerating them, or all the food in the refrigerator will taste like cipolline in agrodolce.

3 tablespoons extra virgin olive oil

2 lbs (907 g) cipollini onions, peeled and kept whole

⅔ cup (158 ml) dry white wine, preferably from the Castelli Romani

3 tablespoons tomato puree from whole canned San Marzano-style tomatoes pureed with a hand blender

6 tablespoons balsamic vinegar

3 tablespoons white wine vinegar

2 tablespoons granulated sugar

10 parsley sprigs, picked and chopped (about 3 tablespoons)

Put the olive oil and onions in a 16-inch (41 cm) sauté pan over medium heat and brown the onions on both sides. Season with salt.

Add the white wine, stir well, and let the liquid reduce by half. Add the tomato puree, mix well to combine, and cook for 2 minutes. Add the vinegars and sugar and stir well. Cover the pan and cook the onions for about 20 minutes or until they are tender, easily pierced with a small knife, and the liquid has reduced by half once again. Add a little water if the mixture begins to dry out. Add the parsley and serve at room temperature or refrigerate.

CONSERVA DI POMODORI
RSFP JARRED TOMATOES

In the last days of July, we gather to jar the bounty of tomatoes that grow in the Bass Garden. I tend to prefer acidic tomatoes for jarring, so I choose early season tomatoes that aren't too sweet, or tomatoes that are naturally acidic. I find that adding only salt, water, and a splash of vinegar is the perfect formula to get the right flavor and texture. Two-quart jars work well here. See page 191 for more on preserving and jarring.

12 to 16 large Roma tomatoes

8 Italian basil leaves

1 tablespoon salt

2 tablespoons red wine vinegar

Bring a large pot of cold water to a boil.

Score the bottom of the tomatoes with an X and core them. When the water comes to a rolling boil, blanch the tomatoes by lowering them, a few at a time, into the water. Let them cook for about 30 seconds, or just long enough for the skins to loosen or blister slightly. Remove the tomatoes quickly using a slotted spoon and transfer them to a bowl of ice water. Peel off the skins with your fingers or with a paring knife.

Bring another large pot of cold water to a boil for the water bath.

Gently pack the tomatoes into a 2-quart (2-l) jar, leaving as little room as possible. Add the salt, vinegar, and basil to the tomatoes and top with a little boiling water to the fill line of the jar. Make sure there are no air bubbles in between the tightly packed tomatoes. Dip the lid in the boiling water and warm it for 30 seconds, then immediately screw the lid onto the jar and firmly tighten it to seal properly.

Process the jarred tomatoes in the boiling water bath for 1 hour. Remove the jar carefully and let it cool on the counter for 24 hours. Store in a cool dark place for up to 1 year.

BASIC RECIPES

AÏOLI

Aïoli is a close cousin of mayonnaise since both are egg- and oil-based emulsions. Mayonnaise is made with whole eggs while aïoli is made with yolks. I would never buy store-bought mayonnaise or aïoli. Filled with preservatives and mystery ingredients, a frightening white color and extremely thick and gloppy, they in no way can compare to the delicious taste, velvety texture, and beautiful yellow color of homemade. Although they may be tricky to prepare the first few times, don't be discouraged—once you get the hang of it, they are quick and easy.

A perfect aïoli should become progressively dense and creamy; at no point should it look like strands of yellow cloth swimming in oil. It is fundamental to whisk constantly and add the oil slowly in a steady trickle, the slower the better, because it allows the oil to be suspended in the lecithin of the yolk. If, after whisking for a long time, the aïoli still hasn't come together, it means that too much oil was added too quickly. In the event that the aïoli has "broken" and the oil and egg aren't coming together, stop adding oil. Sometimes, simply whisking in a drop or two of water can help bring the aïoli back. If that doesn't work, put another yolk in a separate bowl and slowly whisk in the broken aïoli, adding the remaining oil at a trickle. A rule of thumb: use one cup of oil for every egg. However, making a small batch of aïoli with just one egg yolk is much harder than making a bigger batch. Using two egg yolks makes the emulsification process easier.

1 garlic clove	With a mortar and pestle, pound the garlic with a pinch of salt until you obtain a smooth paste.
⅓ cup (79 ml) extra virgin olive oil	
⅔ cup (158 ml) vegetable oil	Combine the olive oil and vegetable oil in a measuring cup.
2 egg yolks	Transfer the garlic paste to a medium bowl and whisk in the egg. Whisking constantly, slowly pour the oil in little by little so that there is a constant trickle. The aïoli will become thicker and a lighter color. If it gets too thick too quickly, add a couple drops of lemon juice. Keep whisking until all of the oil has been added and the aïoli is creamy, opaque, and thick. Keep whisking for about a minute after the aïoli seems emulsified. Taste and adjust the seasoning, adding more lemon juice if you like.
1 teaspoon freshly squeezed lemon juice	

CROSTINI DI PANE
CROUTONS

Lunch and dinner at the American Academy are always served with fresh Lariano-style bread. Lariano bread is originally from the Castelli Romani and is traditionally cooked in a wood-fire oven; it is made with a mixture of whole grain flour and bread flour and is crunchy on the outside and wonderfully fluffy and soft on the inside. We always have leftover bread in the RSFP kitchen, and we make sure to use it all up by making bruschette, large breadcrumbs (for pastas and baked dishes), fine breadcrumbs (for frying), and these croutons, which we use for salads or soups. For a perfectly toasted crouton, it is best to use bread that is a few days old because it will have lost some of its moisture. I like my croutons crunchy on the outside with still a little soft chewiness on the inside, so I taste them often as they toast because they can quickly overcook.

1 pound 4 ounces (567 g) day-old country bread

½ cup (118 ml) extra virgin olive oil

Preheat the oven to 350°F (177 °C).

Carefully remove the crust using a bread knife.

Cut the bread into ½-inch (1.3-cm) cubes.

Toss the bread with the olive oil and season lightly with salt.

Spread the croutons into an even layer on a rimmed baking sheet and bake, stirring and checking every 10 minutes, until the croutons are golden brown and crunchy on the outside and soft on the inside. This should take about 30 minutes.

MOLLICA DI PANE
BREADCRUMBS

Homemade breadcrumbs are extremely versatile. I love them because of the crunch and texture they add to any dish. To my mind, breadcrumbs take dishes to the next level. They are delicious with beans, many types of pasta, salsa verde, and vegetables. This recipe makes about four cups of breadcrumbs. They keep well in an airtight container at room temperature for up to a week.

1 pound 4 ounces day-old country bread (567 g), crust removed

⅓ cup (79 ml) olive oil

Preheat the oven to 300°F (149°C).

Use a food processor to chop the bread into pebble-sized breadcrumbs.

Toss the breadcrumbs with the olive oil and sprinkle with salt to taste.

Spread the breadcrumbs into an even layer on a rimmed baking sheet and bake, stirring and checking every 5 minutes, until the breadcrumbs are perfectly golden brown, about 25 to 35 minutes.

MANDORLE SALATE TOSTATE
TOASTED SALTED ALMONDS

——————

These are our acclaimed RSFP toasted almonds. We sell our homemade salted toasted almonds at the Academy bar, and the community loves them so much that we periodically sell out. These almonds are perfect on their own or chopped up in salads or salsa verde (page 213). They're so easy to make, you'll never want to buy commercially produced salted almonds again. They will keep for up to a month, refrigerated in a sealed container. A word of warning: they are super addictive!

1½ cups almonds	Preheat the oven to 275°F (135°C).
1 teaspoon salt	Dissolve the salt in 2 tablespoons of lukewarm water.
	Put the almonds in a bowl and pour the salty water over them. Stir the almonds until they are all coated in saltwater. Spread them out evenly on a baking sheet lined with parchment paper. Toast the almonds in the oven for about 40 minutes, stirring every 10 minutes. The almonds are ready when they are slightly browned and have a light golden toasted color inching towards the center of the nut. The best way to tell if the almonds are ready is to taste them.

PEPERONI ARROSTITI
ROASTED BELL PEPPERS

I love roasted peppers, and while I prefer to char them over a wood fire, I have found that charring them directly over a gas flame on the stovetop also works wonderfully. I tend not to roast them in an oven, because they often get too soft or over-cooked. If you only have an electric burner or induction stovetop, roast the peppers in the oven at 450°F (232°C). Roasted peppers will keep well for four days, covered, in the refrigerator.

4 red or yellow fleshy bell peppers

1 garlic clove, peeled

3 tablespoons extra virgin olive oil

2 tablespoons red wine vinegar

8 marjoram sprigs, picked and chopped (about 2 teaspoons)

15 parsley sprigs, picked and chopped (about 4 tablespoons)

Place the peppers on the stovetop directly over the gas flame on medium-high heat. Cook them until black and charred on one side, then, using tongs, turn them to the next side. Keep turning until the entire pepper is blistered, black, and charred. Immediately put the peppers in a large bowl and cover it tightly with plastic wrap to steam for 20 minutes.

Cut the peppers in half and scrape out the ribs and seeds, discarding the core. Carefully peel off the skin using the back (not sharp) part of a paring knife by gently scraping off and discarding the black charred skin. Cut the pepper flesh into ½-inch (1.3-cm)-wide strips.

To marinate the peppers, pound the garlic in a mortar and pestle.

In a medium bowl, marinate the bell peppers with the pounded garlic, olive oil, vinegar, herbs, and a large pinch of salt. Taste and adjust the seasoning.

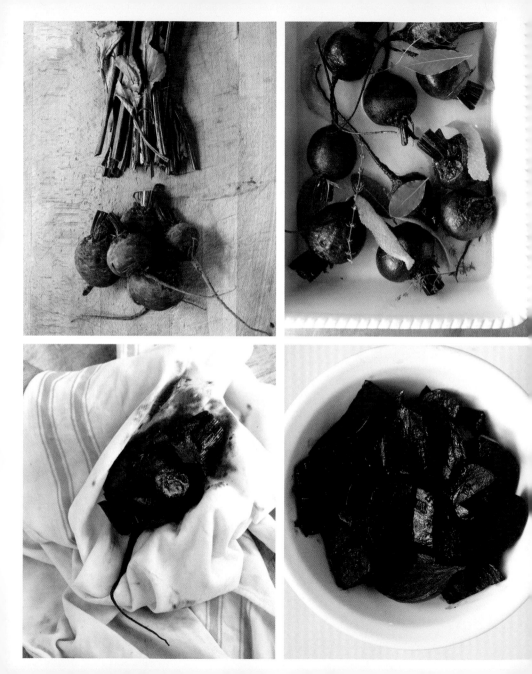

RAPE ROSSE AL FORNO

ROASTED BEETS

Beets aren't particularly common in Italy and you rarely find them fresh. They are sold boiled and vacuum-packed and, quite frankly, are lackluster and not very good. We prefer to grow our own beets in the Bass Garden and select the ones that are just slightly bigger than a golf ball, which showcases their natural sweetness. We broast our beets in a particular way I learned at Chez Panisse, and then marinate them in vinegar, highlighting their sweet and earthy taste and their firm yet yielding texture. These beets have become an RSFP staple, and the community at the Academy loves them. Broasted and marinated beets keep for up to 5 days in the refrigerator.

6 medium beets

2 tablespoons extra virgin olive oil

1 orange

8 thyme sprigs

2 bay leaves

⅓ cup (79 ml) red wine vinegar

Preheat the oven to 400°F (204°C).

Cut the beet tops off, leaving ¼ inch (.6 cm) of stem attached to the beet.

Wash the beets and place them in a deep oven-proof casserole or gratin dish. Toss them with the olive oil and sprinkle liberally with salt.

Using a vegetable peeler, peel 5 or 6 long strips of orange rind.

Add the thyme, bay leaves, and orange peel to the beets and toss well. Add enough water to come ¼ inch (.6 cm) up the sides of the casserole dish. Cover tightly with aluminum foil so no heat or steam escapes, and bake for 40 to 50 minutes, checking every 20 minutes. The beets are done when they are tender when pierced with a knife. They should be neither mushy nor crunchy.

When the beets are cool enough to handle, peel them using your hands, a wet tea towel, or a paring knife. Discard the skins and stems. Cut the beets according to the recipe and marinate them with the red wine vinegar and sprinkle with salt.

SALSA VERDE

There are many versions of this classic salsa throughout Italy, and my favorite includes minced red onions macerated in vinegar. It's so good, you'll want to eat the salsa on its own. In Rome, salsa verde is usually made without onions and instead relies on lemon zest and lemon juice for brightness. It is excellent on poached chicken or boiled beef. We always adapt our salsa verde depending on the season or what we have available. Feel free to experiment with different herbs, like marjoram, chervil, tarragon, chives, or savory, and try using lemon juice instead of red wine vinegar.

3 large shallots or 1 small red onion, peeled and minced (about ½ cup)

½ cup (118 ml) red wine vinegar

½ bunch parsley, picked and chopped (about 1 cup)

20 thyme sprigs, picked and chopped (about 2 tablespoons)

1 mint sprig, picked and chopped (about 1 teaspoon)

½ cup salt-packed capers, rinsed and chopped (p. 229)

1 cup (237 ml) extra virgin olive oil

Macerate the shallots or onions by submerging them in the red wine vinegar. Add a pinch of salt and let sit for 45 minutes.

Combine the remaining ingredients in a medium bowl. Add the macerated onions with a spoon (adding only some of the vinegar) and stir well to combine. Taste and adjust the seasoning with salt and more vinegar from the macerated onions if necessary. The salsa should be balanced with little bites of onion that add brightness and open up the other flavors.

'NDUJA
SPICY CALABRIAN SAUSAGE
————

Calabrians use chilies much like we use salt and pepper. They love to add this spicy sausage to almost any dish: they put 'nduja on vegetables, in pastas, soups, and of course they love it on a bruschetta. This sausage is traditionally made with an equally high percentage of spicy chilies and fat and then lightly smoked by hanging it next to a fire. The spicy chilies are high in ascorbic acid and act as a natural preservative. 'Nduja's high fat content makes it very soft and spreadable. I recommend using a food processor to obtain the almost creamy-like texture of this soft sausage. When you put it in a pan it should actually melt into a red oil that has only a few bits of meat. A spicy little red chili called a diavoletto, or little devil, is traditionally used for 'nduja, but if you can't find them, a fresh cayenne or Fresno chili will work just as well. If you really love spicy food, use the hottest red chili you can find.

1 fresh red hot pepper, like a diavoletto, cayenne, or Fresno hot pepper

1 roasted red pepper, not marinated (see p. 209)

¼ lb (113 g) pure diced or ground pork fat or lard

¼ lb (113 g) finely ground pork shoulder

Put all the ingredients in a food processor and mix until you obtain a smooth paste.

Put this mixture in a 10-inch (25-cm) sauté pan over medium-low heat and cook for just 2 or 3 minutes, until the fat has melted. Transfer the mix to a small loaf pan to let it cool. When the mixture is cool, it will set up due to its high fat content. You then can spread it on toasts, and it will melt on warm vegetables.

BESCIAMELLA
BÉCHAMEL SAUCE

Béchamel is one of the traditional five mother sauces of French cuisine (the others are hollandaise, tomate, espagnole, and velouté). Its origins, however, are Italian: béchamel comes from the Italian word besciamella. In Italy, written records of cooks making besciamella can be traced back to the Middle Ages, yet it isn't until after Catherine de' Medici's reign in France during the 16th century, when the Florentine queen introduced the French to Italian foods and dining customs, that the first records of French béchamel appear. For gratin dishes I like my besciamella on the thicker side, so I use a bit of a higher ratio of roux, the butter and flour mixture, to liquid.

4 tablespoons (57 g) butter

2 oz (57 g) all-purpose flour

3 cups (710 ml) whole milk

Freshly grated nutmeg, to taste

Melt the butter in a small saucepan over medium-low heat. Add the flour and whisk continuously for 4 minutes over medium heat, until the mixture (the roux) goes from white to opaque but does not turn brown.

Turn the heat to medium-low and add the milk little by little, whisking constantly, and keep whisking until the mixture is smooth and thick, about 20 minutes. It might get thick fairly quickly, but you want to make sure the sauce no longer tastes of flour and this requires a longer cooking time. Season with salt and nutmeg to taste and set aside.

ROMESCO

Don't let the long ingredient list deter you from making this delicious sauce. It's easy to bring together once all the ingredients are ready, and it will last in the refrigerator for up to two weeks. Romesco's nuttiness and spiciness wonderfully complement the smokiness of grilled vegetables, pork, and chicken.

¾ cup whole, blanched toasted almonds (p. 233)

½ cup toasted hazelnuts (p. 233)

3 garlic cloves, peeled

½ cup (118 ml) extra virgin olive oil, plus 1 tablespoon

5 sweet dried chilies (such as ancho or Anaheim), stems and seeds removed

1 large pinch saffron threads

1 cup homemade breadcrumbs (p. 205)

½ cup roasted red peppers, not marinated, diced or pureed in a food processor or with a hand blender (p. 209), (optional)

1½ tablespoons sherry vinegar or red wine vinegar

3 tablespoons tomato puree

½ teaspoon paprika

½ teaspoon chili powder

Preheat the oven to 350°F (177°C).

Grind the almonds and hazelnuts with a mortar and pestle or with a food processor until you obtain a consistency like chunky peanut butter. Set the nuts aside.

In the same mortar and pestle (or food processor), pound the garlic into a paste and add a tablespoon of oil to prevent oxidation.

Toast the dried chilies in the oven for about 4 minutes, or until they are just coloring and fragrant. Watch them carefully; since dried peppers have such a high sugar concentration, they can burn easily. The peppers should have a slightly toasted color, and may or may not be firm (they might still be able to be bent). They will harden or crisp up as they cool. Grind them in a food processor or spice grinder until they turn into a powder. Transfer to a medium bowl.

In a small pot, bring 1½ cups of cold water to a boil and pour the boiling water over the dried chili powder. Let the mixture hydrate for 15 minutes. It will turn into a paste.

Put the saffron threads and ¼ cup water in a small saucepan over very low heat. Bring to a boil and immediately remove it from the heat source. Infuse the saffron for 5 minutes.

Combine the nuts, breadcrumbs, the dried chili paste, and the ½ cup roasted peppers. Add the remaining olive oil, vinegar, tomato puree, paprika, chili powder, the garlic, and the saffron liquid. If the sauce is very thick, add more olive oil or water. Taste and adjust the seasoning.

FAGIOLI

COOKED BEANS

———

This recipe is primarily for fresh beans although it works for dried beans as well. I particularly love the taste and texture of fresh beans, but a hearty bowl of pasta e fagioli made with dried beans during the winter is also delicious. Regardless of the season, I cook with beans year round, fresh and dried.

The trick I've learned is to add lots of olive oil to the beans when they're halfway cooked. This layer of oil results in extraordinarily creamy and unctuous beans. We never add salt at the beginning of cooking because it makes the skins tough and leathery. If you are using dry beans, soak them overnight in lots of water. Then proceed with the recipe, cooking them for about 2 hours instead of 1 hour. I recommend making a big batch of beans and using them throughout the week in different soups, salads, or pasta dishes. A bean puree made with leftover beans is delicious on sandwiches—at the RSFP we love to serve bean puree with new-harvest olive oil and escarole on warm pizza bianca for lunch. You can easily double or triple this recipe.

3 pounds (1.4 kg) fresh Borlotti or cannellini beans, shelled (about 3 cups) or 2 cups dried beans

1 carrot, peeled

1 celery stalk

½ yellow onion, peeled

2 garlic cloves, peeled

1 rosemary sprig

1 sage sprig

¼ cup (59 ml) extra virgin olive oil

Put the beans in a 6-quart (6-l) saucepot over medium-low heat and cover them with 6 cups water. Bring to a simmer, taking care not to boil the beans and skimming the foam off the surface. Add all of the vegetables and herbs after skimming the foam off. After 20 minutes add the olive oil and cook for another 20 minutes, or until the beans are tender (for dried beans, add the olive oil after about an hour of cooking). Season the beans with salt, set them aside, and let them rest for an hour before using them, so they firm up.

BASIC TECHNIQUES

CLEANING ANCHOVIES

Buy salt-packed whole anchovies: they have a far more pure and distinct fish flavor than oil-packed fillets. If you buy a large can, take out as many anchovies as you will need for each recipe, and make sure the remaining anchovies are covered with salt. As long as they are under salt, they keep well in the refrigerator for several months.

Rinse the anchovies under cold water, rubbing them delicately and shaking them in the water to remove the salt and the scales. Rinse and drain them at least five times, until the water is no longer murky, then let the anchovies soak in cool water for 15 to 20 minutes, depending on the size of the fish. This process plumps the anchovy and allows you to easily peel the fillets off the bone. Be careful not to over-plump the anchovies or they will taste water-logged.

After 20 minutes, clean the anchovies in a sink with trickling water. Slip a fingertip into the belly of the anchovy and rinse the cavity, removing the fish guts. Carefully pull one fillet off the spine and rinse it, then gently remove the dorsal and ventral fins. Drape the fillet over the side of a clean bowl to drip dry. Once you've peeled off the first fillet, carefully pull the spine off the second filet. Remove the dorsal and ventral fins once again. Rinse the fillet gently and drape it over the side of the bowl. Use immediately or cover with olive oil until needed. They will keep well in the refrigerator, under oil, for up to 3 days.

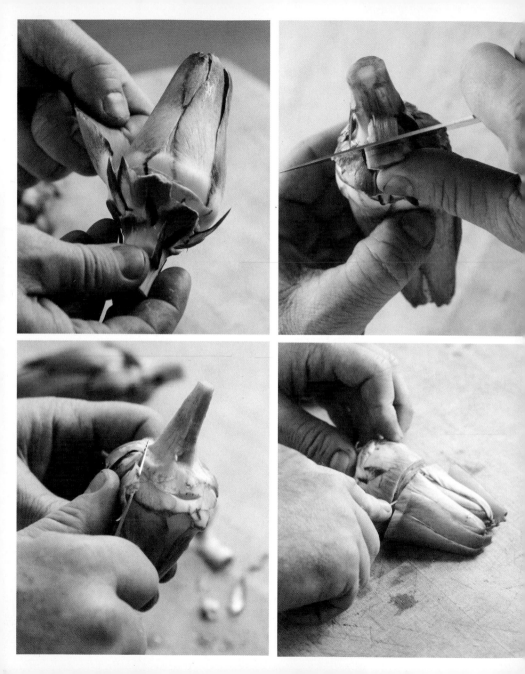

CLEANING ARTICHOKES

Artichokes are labor-intensive to clean—and the yield is small—yet their mesmerizing taste is a reward that makes the effort well worth it. Here in Rome we like to use globe artichokes because they have few or no thorns and they consistently have a more intense flavor than other varietals.

Prepare a large bowl with 1 gallon (3.8 l) of water and squeeze the juice of 1 lemon directly in the bowl; add the lemon halves as well. The acidity of the lemon juice prevents the artichokes from oxidizing and turning dark brown. Handle artichokes as quickly as possible, as they oxidize and turn brown as soon as they are peeled. Snap off the tough outer petals one at a time until you reach the pale colored petals of the heart of the artichoke. Using a small knife, pare away the dark green layer from the stem and around the base of the artichoke (there is a paler green layer underneath). Dip the artichoke in the lemon water and return it to the cutting board. Cut off the top of the artichoke flower to about 1 inch (2.5 cm) above the base. Immediately put the artichoke in the lemon water. Artichokes will keep for up to 24 hours submerged in lemon water.

If you need to slice the artichokes, remove the artichoke from the water and cut it in half lengthwise. Scoop out the choke (fuzzy part of the heart) using a small spoon. Dip the artichoke in the lemon water once again and return it to the board. Slice it according to the recipe you are using and keep in the lemon water until needed.

CLEANING POMEGRANATES

Pomegranates resemble citrus in that they can be divided into segments just like an orange. Fill a bowl with cold water. Cut the pomegranate into quarters along the segment lines. Submerge one of the quarters and carefully remove the seeds with your fingers. Pomegranates squirt lots of juice and cleaning them underwater avoids being stained by indelible pomegranate juice and allows the pith to float to the surface so that it can easily be removed. Skim off the pith and drain the pomegranate seeds.

PEELING GARLIC

Always peel garlic right before you need it. If you prepare it in advance, make sure you cover it with a small amount of olive oil to preserve its flavors and ensure that it does not oxidize. The same goes for sliced or chopped garlic: always cover it with olive oil until you need it.

Remove the cloves from the garlic head. Cut the bottom off the clove and smash it, with the skin on, using either the heel of your palm or the thick part of a chef's knife. Smashing the clove first helps remove the skins easily. Carefully peel away the skin. Pry the clove open with your fingers and remove the germ inside the clove at its center (usually a green sprout, although it can be white). It is important to remove the germ, because it has a different consistency from the rest of the garlic; it can burn easily when cooked and make the oil taste bitter. Keep the garlic under oil until needed.

RINSING CAPERS

Buy salt-packed capers: they have a more intense flavor than brined capers (capers sold in liquid), and the brine itself may interfere with the taste of the dish you're making. Soaking the capers in water removes the salt through a process known as osmosis. Using warm water speeds up this process and allows a lot of salt to be removed in only half an hour instead of the 3 or 4 hours it would take with cold water.

Rinse the capers in a fine-meshed strainer or skimmer until the salt has fallen off. Put the capers in a small pot, cover them with cold water, and place them over low heat. When the water comes to a simmer, turn off the heat and let the capers soak in the hot water for 15 to 20 minutes. Drain the capers in a colander and rinse them under cold water. Taste the capers: if they still seem too salty, repeat this process once or even twice. When the capers are just salty enough, squeeze them dry to remove excess salty water.

PEELING CITRUS

Peeling citrus well with a knife takes some serious practice, but it has a great practical advantage: by removing all the pith, most of the fruit's bitterness is removed, and its sweetness is maximized. It has an aesthetic advantage as well: slices of a perfectly peeled orange or grapefruit make for a beautiful and clean presentation.

On a cutting board, cut off the top and bottom of the citrus to obtain a flat and even cutting surface. Using a sharp knife, carefully peel away the skin of the fruit, from top to bottom, removing the pith and following the segment line of the fruit. Rotate the fruit as you keep peeling so you can always see the white line of the pith, where you should be cutting. Trim away any remaining pith. Slice the citrus and refrigerate until needed.

TOASTING NUTS

Toasting nuts brings out complexity in their flavor and makes walnuts and hazelnuts easier to peel. I like to break the nuts in half to see their color and taste them at several intervals as they are toasting to make sure they don't toast too much. The nuts will continue to toast after they are taken out of the oven because their oil stores residual heat, so remove them from the oven when you see a light golden color inching towards the center of the nut and when they have a crunchy and richer "nuttier" taste.

Preheat the oven to 300°F (149°C).

Spread the nuts evenly on a rimmed baking sheet and toast them for 10 minutes, or until the skins begin to split and the nuts are fragrant. While the nuts are still warm, place them inside a clean tea towel. Gather the towel into a secure bundle and roll the nuts in a circular motion to loosen and remove some of the skins, and with them any extra bitterness. Lift the nuts out of the towel, leaving behind the skins. If you like, sift them through a strainer, shaking the nuts to remove any remaining skins. Pine nuts, because they have no skin, need a little less time to toast. Try toasting them for 7 minutes, or until they just start to turn light golden brown.

WASHING LETTUCE & CHICORIES

Buy whole heads of lettuce or bunches at a local farmers' market or good grocery store. Whole heads are superior to bagged leaves in quality, taste, and nutritional value. Steer clear of bagged lettuce: it presents environmental problems and raises health concerns. Bagged greens are washed up to five times, wasting huge amounts of water. Bagged leaves also cost far more than whole heads of lettuce. You must also think about what is sprayed on bagged greens to give them such a long shelf life. Lettuce kept in a plastic bag isn't able to breathe and rots after three days.

Washing lettuce is something I feel very strongly about because I find that it is so rarely done correctly. Trimming and washing the leaves properly is of the utmost importance. Here are the steps to follow for perfectly washed lettuce:

Pull off and discard any outer leaves that are rough, torn, or discolored. Always be gentle with the lettuce. You should have a compact head with healthy delicious-looking leaves.

If the leaves are small and tender, leave them whole. Otherwise, tear the leaves into bite-sized pieces, or cut the lettuce lengthwise into small ribbons.

Drop the lettuce into a deep sink or large bowl filled with very cold water. Cold water helps to refresh the lettuce and crisp it. A wilted head of lettuce will revive after 30 minutes in cold water. Shake the lettuce in the water to remove any dirt that is stuck to the leaves. Let sit for 15 minutes so that any dirt settles at the bottom of the sink or bowl, making sure that there is enough water to allow the lettuce to float well above the bottom of the bowl or sink.

Gently remove the lettuce from the water and place it in a strainer making sure not to disturb the water as you remove the lettuce; the dirt should remain settled on the sink floor. Drain the sink water, rinsing away the dirt, and fill the sink or bowl again with very cold water. Add the lettuce and wash it again. Repeat this process until all the dirt has been removed from the lettuce.

Remove the lettuce from the water and dry it in a salad spinner or by laying it out to air dry on clean dishtowels. Use the lettuce right away or store it in the refrigerator wrapped in dishtowels.

BIBLIOGRAPHY

Artusi, Pellegrino, and Piero Camporesi. *La scienza in cucina e l'arte di mangiar bene*. Torino: G. Einaudi, 2001.

Ball Blue Book Guide to Preserving. Daleville, IN: Hearthmark LLC, 2009.

Bertolli, Paul. *Chez Panisse Cooking*. New York, NY: Random House, 1988.

Bertolli, Paul, Gail Skoff, and Judy Dater. *Cooking by Hand*. New York: Clarkson Potter, 2003.

Boswell, Christopher. *Pasta: Recipes from the Kitchen of the American Academy in Rome, the Rome Sustainable Food Project*. New York: The Little Bookroom, 2013.

Bugialli, Giuliano, and Andy Ryan. *Giuliano Bugialli's Foods of Naples and Campania*. New York: Stewart, Tabori & Chang, 2003.

Bugialli, Giuliano. *The Fine Art of Italian Cooking*. New York: Times, 1989.

Cesari, Monica Saroni. *Italy Dish by Dish*. Trans. Susan Simon. New York: The Little Bookroom, 2011.

Clark, Sam, and Sam Clark. *Moro: The Cookbook*. London: Ebury, 2001.

Coleman, Eliot. *Four-Season Harvest: Organic Vegetables from your Home Garden All Year Around*. White River Junction, Vt.: Chelsea Green Pub., 1999.

Coleman, Eliot. *The New Organic Grower: A Master's Manual of Tools and Techniques for the Home and Market Gardener*. Rev. and expanded ed. White River Junction, Vt.: Chelsea Green Pub. Co., 1995.

Downie, David. *Cooking the Roman Way: Authentic Recipes from the Home Cooks and Trattorias of Rome*. New York: Harper Collins, 2002.

Gho, Paola. *The Slow Food Dictionary to Italian Regional Cooking*. Bra, Italy: Slow Food Editor, 2010.

McGee, Harold. *Food and Cooking: An Encyclopedia of Kitchen Science, History and Culture*. London: Hodder and Stoughton, 2004.

Ottolenghi, Yotam, and Jonathan Lovekin. *Plenty*. London: Ebury, 2010.

Ottolenghi, Yotam, Sami Tamimi, and Richard Learoyd. *Ottolenghi: The Cookbook*. London: Ebury, 2008.

Plotkin, Fred. *Italy for the Gourmet Traveler*. Boston: Little, Brown, 1996.

Pollan, Michael. *The Omnivore's Dilemma: A Natural History of Four Meals*. New York: Penguin Press, 2006.

Riley, Gillian. *The Oxford Companion to Italian Food*. Oxford: Oxford UP, 2007.

Riotte, Louise. *Carrots Love Tomatoes: Secrets of Companion Planting for Successful Gardening*. Pownal, VT: Storey Pub., 1998.

Rodgers, Judy. *The Zuni Café Cookbook*. New York: W. W. Norton, 2002.

Slow Food Editore. *L'Orto in Cucina*. Bra: Slow Food Editore, 2012.

Talbott, Mona and Mirella Misenti. *Biscotti: Recipes from the Kitchen of the American Academy in Rome*. New York: The Little Bookroom, 2010.

Talbott, Mona. *Zuppe: Soups from the Kitchen of the American Academy in Rome, the Rome Sustainable Food Project*. New York: The Little Bookroom, 2012.

The Silver Spoon. New York: Phaidon Press, 2005.

Waters, Alice, David Tanis, and Fritz Streiff. *Chez Panisse Café Cookbook*. New York: HarperCollins, 1999.

Waters, Alice. *Chez Panisse Vegetables*. New York: HarperCollins Publishers, 1996.

Waters, Alice. *The Art of Simple Food*. New York: Clarkson Potter, 2007.

Zanini de Vita, Oretta, Maureen B. Fant, and Howard M. Isaacs. *The Food of Rome and Lazio: History, Folklore, and Recipes*. Rome, Italy: Alphabyte, 1994.

RECIPE INDEX

ACKNOWLEDGEMENTS

I would like to acknowledge and thank the following people for their extraordinary efforts that made this book possible.

Adele Chatfield-Taylor, AAR President and CEO, Christopher Celenza, AAR Director, the AAR Trustees, and the American Academy staff for their help and support during this process. The *dipendenti* are an infinite source of knowledge, passion, and *buone forchette* that have forever made a profound impact on how I cook and eat.

The Fellows, Affiliated Fellows, fellow travelers, Residents, and visitors at the American Academy that I have met in my seven years here. To cook for such a talented community of impassioned people is a privilege that makes all the hard work worth it.

Angela Hederman and the Little Bookroom for their continued faith and support in the RSFP and our efforts to share our kitchen's recipes and philosophy.

Annie Schlechter for her amazing photography, patience, and vision. Annie's ability to capture all these difficult shots so effortlessly, to make people relax and enjoy themselves, helped the process seem more life fun than work.

Elena Goldblatt for her tireless work ethic, thoughtfulness, and commitment not only to this project but to the RSFP as a whole. Her dedication to this book while working a full-time job gave me courage to dig deeper when I thought I couldn't. Your miracle work with my words has been a godsend. Thanks G.

Russell Maret for his continued loyalty to produce the unbelievable fonts for all the RSFP cookbooks, his countless trips to the various shops and stores to get equipment or supplies for us, general overall cheery disposition, and those amazing (and rather necessary) cocktails after 15-hour work days.

Laura Offeddu for all her hard work, kind words of encouragement, and support.

Chris Behr for being a tremendous ally, friend, teacher, and hell of a great cook, who helped lead this team wonderfully through thick and thin, while showing tremendous vision, resolve, and creativity.

Francesca Strazzullo for countless lessons and insight on Italian culture and food, and teaching me how Italians both eat and ate. I can only hope to have passed on a tenth of what you gave to me.

The recipe testers who took the time to give me feedback on all these recipes; it was so important to me that they translate both in Italy and America, and thanks to you all this is a reality.

The RSFP staff, Gabriel Soare, Alessandro Lima, Tiziana Del Grosso, Tewelde Weldekidan, Tesfamichel Ghebrehawareit, Mirella Misenti, and Federico Madonna for their patience and support throughout this whole process, and their undying loyalty.

The 2012-2013 interns: Leigh Hartman, Julie Stelmaszyk, Cameron Cox, Daniel Etherington, Ross Phillips, Sara Levi, Marlon Fernandes, Nathan Gilmour, Alice Shields, Tom Lee, Sean Loria, Kelly Mariani, Mary Eliabeth Krall, Florence Clarke, Oliver Monday, Natalie Gullish, and Jacqueline McKay.

Adele Chatfield-Taylor and Alice Waters, thank you for starting this wonderful collaboration, it has been a dream come true for me to come back to the food, culture, and country that I cherish so dearly. I hope these books help cement a foundation that you both envisioned for this delicious revolution.

Mona Talbott and Alice Waters for choosing, trusting, believing in me, and being there every step of the way. It is a true honor to be your colleague and follow in your footsteps.

Above all, I would like to thank my family for convincing me that I am a cook.

Christopher Boswell
Rome

AMERICAN ACADEMY IN ROME

The American Academy in Rome is a center for independent study and advanced research in the arts and humanities. For more than 116 years the Academy has offered support, time and an inspiring environment to some of America's most gifted artists and scholars. Each year, through a national juried competition, the Academy offers up to thirty Rome prize fellowships in architecture, literature, musical composition, visual arts, and in humanistic approaches to ancient studies, medieval studies, Renaissance and early modern studies, and modern Italian studies. Fellows are joined by a select group of Residents, distinguished artists and scholars invited by the Director. Many Academy Fellows and Residents have had a significant influence in the world of art, music, culture, literature, scholarship and education.

Founded in 1894, the Academy was charted as a private institution by an act of Congress in 1905. The Academy remains a private institution supported by gifts from individuals, foundations and corporations, and the membership of colleges, universities and arts and cultural organizations, as well as by grants from the National Endowment for the Humanities and the United States Department of Education.

www.aarome.org

THE ROME SUSTAINABLE
FOOD PROJECT

The Rome Sustainable Food Project, a program devoted to providing organic, local and sustainable meals for the community of the American Academy in Rome, has launched a delicious revolution to rethink institutional dining. Headed by chef Mona Talbott, a Chez Panisse alum, and guided by Alice Waters, the menus have given rise to a new, authentic cuisine, inspired by *la cucina romana*, Chez Panisse, and the collective experience of those working in the AAR kitchen. A logical extension of the Academy's values, since its official launch in February 2007, the Rome Sustainable Food Project has transformed the community of the American Academy in Rome with a collaborative dining program that nourishes and supports both work and conviviality and aims to construct a replicable model for sustainable dining in an institution.

ABOUT THE AUTHOR

Christopher Boswell is the Executive Chef of the Rome Sustainable Food Project and the author of the previous cookbook in the RSFP series, *Pasta*. He has been at the RSFP since the program was established in 2006, when he was chosen by Alice Waters to work with former RSFP Executive Chef Mona Talbott.

Boswell started out as a dishwasher and a prep cook in the small gold rush town of Jackson, California. After high school, he attended the California Culinary Academy where he received the distinguished Daniel Carlisle Walker award for culinary excellence. He then went on to work at Stars, Acquarello, and One Market restaurants before moving to Italy for a year to learn authentic rustic cooking.

Chef Boswell then joined Chez Panisse, where he received five years of intensive training under Alice Waters and her brigade of distinguished chefs.

Elena Goldblatt moved from Canada to her mother's native Rome when she was 12 years old and has been drawn back ever since. She graduated from Yale University in 2010 and was an intern in the Rome Sustainable Food Project kitchen in 2011. She has worked for author and journalist Mark Bittman at *The New York Times* and for Monica Larner at *The Wine Advocate*. Elena has collaborated with Chef Christopher Boswell on the RSFP cookbooks *Pasta* and *Verdure*.

ABOUT THE PHOTOGRAPHER

Annie Schlechter is a New Yorker and has been working as a photographer since 1998. Her clients include: *New York Magazine, The World of Interiors, Veranda, Coastal Living, Travel + Leisure* and many more but she adores working on projects with *The Little Bookroom*.